THE YOUNG JAMES BARRIE

Also by Michael Elder
THE YOUNG LUTHER

The Young
James Barrie

MICHAEL ELDER

Illustrated by Susan Gibson

A MAX PARRISH BOOK
MACDONALD : LONDON
&
ROY PUBLISHERS INC. : NEW YORK 10021

PUBLISHED IN GREAT BRITAIN BY
MACDONALD AND CO LTD, 49/50 POLAND STREET, LONDON W.1

PUBLISHED IN THE U.S.A. BY
ROY PUBLISHERS INC. 30 EAST 74TH STREET NEW YORK
N.Y. 10021

Library of Congress Catalog Card Number 68–22704
© Michael Elder 1968
SBN 356 02410 5
Printed in Great Britain by
W. & G. Baird Limited, Belfast

Contents

Chairs

Nanny Matthew trotted down the road, one hand firmly clutching her carpet bag, the other holding her skirts clear of the dust which swirled around her feet in this hot weather. Her face was flushed, happy and eager-looking, as though she had some great secret which she was longing to pass on to someone. As she went busily down the road towards the dip where the houses descended to the Gairie Burn she was humming contentedly to herself one of the psalm tunes she had heard in the kirk the previous Sunday.

It was a bonny day near the beginning of May with a few fleecy white clouds hanging still in the blue sky, and the early morning light which flooded Kirriemuir lit up the red stone houses in a deep soft glow. In the distance to the south the blue humps of the Sidlaw Hills seemed to quiver in the haze, and to the north the foothills of the Grampians were sharply cut against the sky.

She heard the slow clip-clop of hooves before the carrier's cart turned the corner coming towards her, the old horse bowed and straining between the shafts as he dragged the cart up the slight rise.

Nanny Matthew stopped as she drew abreast of the cart, and the carrier, sitting crouched at the front with the reins drooping between his fingers said gently:

'Whoa!'

The horse obediently stopped, but not before he had drawn the cart in to the road edge where he could crop the grass at the verge while his master gossiped.

'Aye, Geordie,' said Nanny Matthew.

'Aye, Nanny,' said Geordie. 'It's all over then?'

'Aye. Just half an hour ago,' said Nanny.

'Is all well?'

'Fine, man, fine. Couldna be better.'

'What was it?'

'A boy, Geordie. A fine healthy boy.'

'The Lord be thanked,' said Geordie devoutly. 'And how's Margaret?'

'She's fine.'

Nanny Matthew stepped closer to the cart, her eyes sparkling and her whole expression showing that she was about to tell some enormous secret.

'And ye ken what, Geordie?' she said excitedly.

'No. What?'

'They're goin' tae call the bairn after me!'

'Eh? Call a boy Nanny?' echoed Geordie in astonishment.

'Och, dinna be daft, Geordie! Of course not. They're goin' tae call him by my last name!'

Geordie squinted down at her and considered carefully for some time.

'Matthew Barrie,' he said at last slowly, as though he were tasting the name and found it not very much to his liking.

"Well, no. Not exactly,' Nanny admitted somewhat reluctantly. 'It's tae be the laddie's middle name.'

'Aye. That's better,' said Geordie with considerable relief. 'I doubt Matthew Barrie doesna sound quite right. What's his forename tae be?'

'James,' said Nanny.

Geordie considered this again at some length.

'James Matthew Barrie,' he said. He smacked his lips and repeated the name as though to give it another chance. 'Aye. Aye, well, mebbe that's not sae bad.'

'It's good,' said Nanny. 'And I told Margaret that. "With a name like yon, Margaret," says I, "there's nae sayin' where the laddie may end up," says I.'

'Did they not give the name tae one of the other bairns?' said Geordie.

A shadow passed over Nanny Matthew's face.

'Aye,' she said. 'They did. Poor wee Agnes. Agnes Matthew Barrie. Her that only lived a month. She died in 1851. That's nine years back. Mercy, how the days fly by!'

'Aye, I mind that,' said Geordie.

'Well, they've not forgot me, I'm glad tae say,' said Nanny briskly. 'Me that's been at the birth of all the

Barrie bairns. And I'm glad there's one that'll carry my name.'

She smoothed down the front of her dress and shook out her skirts so that they hung properly again. Having told her great secret she now had time to look round at the load on the cart behind Geordie. It seemed bulky, but she could make nothing of it, for it was covered with a sacking sheet.

'Are ye for the Tenements yourself, Geordie?' she asked.

Geordie nodded.

'Aye,' he said, and he jerked his head towards the load in the cart without looking round. 'That's them.'

Nanny Matthew took a step towards the back of the cart.

'Could I just hae a wee peep, dae ye think?' she asked.

'No,' said Geordie. 'They're well wrapped up and I'm no' wantin' them undone before I get there. They might get dusty and I doubt David Barrie wouldna like that.'

Nanny Matthew nodded reluctantly.

'Aye. Well, mebbe ye're right, Geordie,' she said. 'I'd like fine tae hae a wee look, but I'll see them later when I call back at the Tenements. Are they bonny?'

'Ye might say sae,' said Geordie without much enthusiasm.

'I'm sure they will be. Margaret was gettin' intae quite a state about them. Almost as soon as the bairn was born she says tae me, "Are they here yet, Nanny?" "No," says I. "I've not heard them comin'." "Slip out tae the Brechin Road and see of ye can see any sign of them," says she —'

Geordie roused himself as it seemed that this story might go on for some time.

'Aye, well,' he said, 'if I dinna get them up there soon

she'll mebbe be out in the Brechin Road lookin' for them herself. Forebye, I've other places tae call at this day. I'll need tae be movin'. Good day tae ye, Nanny.'

He slapped the reins along the horse's back and clicked at him through his teeth. The horse raised his head from the verge, blades of succulent green grass hanging from his mouth, and leant against the shafts. Slowly the cart began to creak and move forward, the iron-rimmed wheels rumbling on the gravel of the road. Nanny Matthew watched them go and then turned and hurried on along the road to the town to find someone else to tell her great secret to.

Geordie the carrier sat almost motionless as the horse drew the cart along the Brechin Road. To the right stood a row of cottages, and to the left a grassy bank with beyond it the severe outline of the Auld Licht Manse. A little further along Geordie pulled on the right hand rein and the horse obediently turned and headed into Lilybank, a narrow passage between two houses.

The cart echoed and rumbled through the gap and emerged into a wide yard. A pull on the left rein turned the horse again and Geordie drew to a halt outside a door.

It was the first house in a row of plain, no-nonsense houses with small windows on either side of the door and two further windows upstairs, and a grey slate roof surmounted by two chimney pots. A tall man would have to duck his head to get through the front door, and a very tall man might not be able to stand upright in the low rooms inside without bumping his head on the rafters, but the house was neat, trim and as clean as a new pin.

The sound of the cart rumbling on the cobbles of the yard brought a sudden torrent of people pouring out of the door. As Geordie stepped stiffly down from his seat and made his way to the back of the cart to undo the covering sheet, he recognised them as they came. The biggest girl was Mary. She was fifteen. Then came Jane Ann, thirteen years old and the quiet, capable one of the family. After them came the bouncing, cheerful seven-year-old David and five-year-old Sara.

Behind them, stooping through the doorway, came David Barrie senior, a big, powerful man with a dark beard flecked with grey and a broad face which might have been stern if it had not been for the twinkle of humour in his eyes. He held the hand of the round, unsteady form of Isabella who was nearly three.

'Good day, Geordie,' he said as his children ran round the cart, scrambling on to the tailboard and shouting excitedly to each other – all except Isabella who stood to one side near her father and watched round-eyed the antics of her older brother and sisters which she could not yet share.

'Good day tae ye, David,' said Geordie. 'How's Margaret?'

'She's fine, thank ye,' said Mr Barrie. 'Ye'll hae heard the news?'

'Aye. I met Nanny Matthew on my way.'

'Mphm. Then ye'll ken all,' said Mr Barrie, his face serious but his eyes laughing.

'Hey, you bairns! Mind what ye're daein' on the cart!' shouted Geordie. 'Ye dinna want tae spoil them!'

'Mary, keep the bairns away, will ye?' said Mr Barrie. 'They can watch, but they're not tae interfere.'

'All right, Father,' said Mary and she began to persuade the others to leave the cart and stand aside to watch while Geordie and their father unwrapped the precious load.

Off came the sacking sheet, and Geordie and Mr Barrie climbed into the cart and began to untie the wrappings round one of the objects lying on the floor-boards. The children watching saw that their father's face seemed unnaturally pale, but they knew that this was from excitement.

The first of the shapeless objects was unwrapped, and there, exposed in the sunlight, was a chair. A hair-bottomed chair, its woodwork glowing in the sun, and the children gasped with delight. David Barrie stood looking at it, one hand on his hip, the other stroking his beard and there was a light of satisfaction in his face. He slowly walked round the chair standing on the cobbles, viewing it from all angles.

'That's braw,' he said softly at last. 'Are they not braw, Geordie?'

'Aye,' said Geordie grudgingly. 'They're not bad for second hand.'

'One pound seven shillings and sixpence, the six of them cost,' said Mr Barrie. 'It took a long time tae save that much, but they're worth every penny of it.'

'Aye,' said Geordie. 'I'll get the others unwrapped if ye'll carry them in.'

David Barrie gently picked up the first chair and, as though he were walking on eggshells, carried it very carefully to the door. He slid it gently through, taking care not to scratch the door's paintwork and even more care not to scratch the chair itself.

There was a little square lobby beyond the entrance door. Two doors led off on either side, and directly ahead a short flight of stairs led up to the rooms above. Mr Barrie took the chair carefully through to the room on the right, laying it tenderly on the floor in a place

where none of the children were likely to trip over it
and nothing would accidentally bump against it.

As he stood looking at the new chair standing alone
in the middle of the floor he heard a call from upstairs.

'Is that them, David?' called a woman's voice.

'Aye, Margaret, they've come,' he called back.

'Oh, I must see them!'

There was an ominous creak from the room upstairs
and David Barrie hurried to the door and called up.

'Now, you bide where ye are! Ye're not fit tae be
traipsin' round the house yet! The chairs will keep!'

'But I want tae see my chairs, David.'

'Ye'll see your chairs soon enough, woman!'

'Are they bonny?'

David Barrie considered the chair for a moment
through the open door of the room he had just left.

'Aye,' he called. 'Aye, Margaret. They're bonny, right
enough.'

He turned and went out into the yard again. Geordie
by now had the other five chairs standing on the cobbles
with their wrappings off, and the children were circling
round them, staring at them as though they were some
strange animals that they longed to stroke but did not
quite dare.

'Jane Ann, will ye go tae your mother,' said Mr
Barrie. 'She's fair desperate tae see the chairs, and I
doubt she'll be down the stairs before we can stop her if
there's not someone tae keep an eye on her.'

Jane Ann came obediently forward.

'Aye, Father, I'll go tae her,' she said quietly, and with
a last longing look at the chairs standing in the yard she
turned and hurried into the house.

'And make sure your wee brother's all right,' Mr

Barrie called after her. 'The state she's in, she's thinkin'
more of the chairs than she is of him.'

'Can I carry one of the chairs in, Father, please can
I?' asked young David eagerly.

Mr Barrie shook his head.

'No, David,' he said. 'Ye'd best leave that tae Mary
and me. Then if any of them gets damaged it's our fault
and no one else's.'

Young David's face fell, and Mr Barrie rumpled the
thick curly dark hair as he saw his disappointment.

'Never mind, son,' he said gently. 'Later on I'll let ye
sit in one of them.'

Young David let out a whoop of pleasure and went
tearing into the house. They heard his feet clattering
up the stairs to his mother's room.

Mr Barrie smiled at his oldest daughter.

'Come on, then, Mary,' he said. 'Let's take them in.
But go carefully, now.'

'Aye, Father,' said Mary.

One by one they carried the chairs into the room to
the right of the entrance door. When they were all in
Mr Barrie had a moment of doubt. There seemed to be
very little space left. So little room and so many children in the house. Something would have to be done
about that. James brought the number living in the
house to eight, and there was also the oldest boy, Alexander, who came home during the holidays from Aberdeen University.

He spent a little while arranging the chairs so that
they would be as much out of the way as possible, but
even so they were bound to get damaged sooner or later.

The doorway darkened suddenly as Geordie poked
his head in.

'I'll away then,' he said.

Mr Barrie came back to earth with a start.

'Right, Geordie, thank ye,' he said.

Geordie surveyed the room critically.

'Ye're a wee thing pressed for space now,' he observed, and he left the house and clumped across the yard to the horse and cart standing patiently waiting.

The clatter of the horse's hooves and the rumble of the iron-tyred wheels on the cobbles brought all the children running out of the house again to watch the carrier leave.

They waved goodbye as the cart headed into Lily-bank, and young David ran after it until it turned into the Brechin Road and set off towards the centre of Kirriemuir. Then he came strutting back, hands thrust into the pockets of his knickerbockers, whistling gaily, the proud owner of six new chairs, one of which he was shortly going to be allowed to sit in.

For a minute or two Mr Barrie and the children stood in the yard, and then suddenly they all began to move towards the house, the new chairs beckoning to them, the children scampering ahead of Mr Barrie, except for Isabella who took his hand and staggered along beside him.

At the doorway to the room Jane Ann, who was ahead of the rest, stopped with a little cry.

'Mother!' she said accusingly. 'You *promised!*'

Margaret Ogilvy rose guiltily to her feet, and Jane Ann ran to help her as she swayed slightly. She was a small woman with a gentle face with strongly marked crow's feet at the corners of her eyes, showing that she laughed a lot. Just now she looked pale and tired. She was dressed in a long linen nightdress which made her look a little helpless.

'I only came down for a moment,' she said.

'Meaning that ye havena really been here at all, eh?'
said Mr Barrie with mock severity which was tinged
with worry. 'Margaret, ye're not strong enough yet tae
be gallivantin' up and down the stairs like that.'

'I ken, David, but I couldna rest till I'd seen my
chairs. And see, David, there's a wee scratch on the leg
of this one. I found it. See?'

For a moment their attention was turned away from
her as they all crowded to look at the tiny, almost invisible scratch on the leg of one of the chairs.

'That's nothing,' said Mr Barrie at last, and they
could all hear the relief in his voice. 'A wee bit polish
will soon hide that. Now, will one of you bairns get your
mother's shawl and see that she goes back tae her bed
and bides there?'

There was a rush to find the shawl which was placed
round their mother's shoulders, and then the children
escorted her out of the room and up the stairs to her bed,
Mary carrying Isabella and Jane Ann helping their
mother, while David ran on ahead and Sara brought up
the rear.

Mr Barrie stayed downstairs, listening to the thumps
and bangs from the bedroom above, hearing the protests of his wife as she said she had not meant to come
down, and anyway she was feeling perfectly all right,
and in fact she was a lot better now that she had actually
seen the chairs, and now she would be able to rest in
comfort and give her attention to little James who was
sleeping peacefully in the cradle and quite obviously
hadn't missed her at all, and what a lot of fuss about
nothing, anyway.

Mr Barrie smiled and shook his head and sighed, and
then set about pushing the chairs around again, trying
to find the best place for them.

A little later there was a rap at the outside door and a woman's voice shouted in:

'Are ye there, Margaret Ogilvy?'

Mr Barrie strode to the door which stood open. Standing on the threshold was a small woman leaning heavily on a stick, carrying a bowl in her other hand.

'It's yourself, Bell Lunan,' said Mr Barrie.

'Good morning, David,' said Bell Lunan. 'How is Margaret?'

'She's fine.'

'And the bairn?'

'Sleepin' peaceful, I hear.'

'My, that's grand. I've brought Margaret a wee thing of calves' foot jelly, which will help tae bring back her strength. And ye've got the chairs, I see.'

'There's not much ye miss, Bell.'

'Och, no. I can sit at my wee window next door there and see all of life that passes by. I saw Geordie come and go, so I kent the chairs were here.'

'Come away in, then, and ye can see the chairs and Margaret – and the bairn as well.'

'Thank ye.'

Bell Lunan hobbled into the house and stood at the door of the room admiring the chairs, and a little later David Barrie helped her slowly up the stairs to see Margaret.

She lay in the bed with the cradle beside her, and David Barrie chased the children out and left the two old friends together to talk, closing the door quietly behind him.

Bell Lunan looked closely at the sleeping child, his eyes screwed up tight, one tiny fist clenched outside the blanket.

'He takes after his father, Margaret,' said Bell.

Margaret smiled gently.

'Aye,' she said. 'He'll be a bonny man one day.'

'It's a pity he'll not be able tae hae a college education like Alexander,' said Bell.

Margaret smiled again.

'What makes ye say that?' she asked.

'Well, the way the handloom weavin's goin' these days, I doubt David'll not be able tae afford it,' said Bell. 'He's done gey well sendin' his oldest boy tae the University at Aberdeen.'

Margaret did not reply, but turned the talk to the new chairs in the downstairs room. A little later young James stirred in the cradle and the little fists opened and then tightened again. He began to cry.

Margaret turned in the bed.

'Could ye hand him tae me, Bell?' she asked.

Bell Lunan laid her stick on the floor within reach, gathered the tiny bundle carefully into her arms and passed it across to Margaret. Then she lowered herself into her chair again and picked up her stick. Margaret cradled her son and made soothing noises and in a minute he quietened and fell asleep again. Margaret continued to rock him softly backwards and forwards, crooning gently to him, her words inaudible to Bell. Then suddenly she raised her voice slightly, and though she was still only speaking to the child, Bell Lunan could hear what she said quite clearly.

'No college education for my wee laddie?' she said. 'Well, Jamie, you and me will see about that!'

2

Giant

With the arrival of James, the Barrie children numbered seven and before very long it had risen to eight, for two years later the Barries had another daughter, called Margaret after her mother. This did not include the two children who had died very young, the two girls, Elizabeth and Agnes, who lay buried in the Hill Cemetery which overlooked Kirriemuir.

Soon after James's birth there were changes in the

Tenements. James never knew, as the older children did, the sound of his father's loom clicking away from dawn till dusk in the downstairs room to the left of the outside door, because now it was quite clear to Mr Barrie that with seven children and six new chairs the house was too crowded, so he moved his loom to a house a little distance away.

This meant that Margaret now had four rooms in her home, and this seemed a luxury indeed. To be sure, the Barrie's house at the Tenements was bigger than most handloom weavers' houses, and now that Mr Barrie's loom was moved away it seemed even bigger. Most of the weavers had only a but and ben, a two room cottage with the loom in one room and the other for living in.

Now Margaret was able to make a real parlour in the downstairs room where the loom had been, and into this room, with loving care, she moved the hair-bottomed chairs.

The house was quiet with the departure of the loom. The family had grown so used to the click of the shuttle, to seeing their father through the window as they played in the yard outside, bent over his linen weaving all day and every day – except Sundays, of course.

They were proud men, the Kirriemuir handloom weavers. The linen they wove may not have been as delicate as that woven by the men of Paisley or Glasgow, but it was just as important. It was mostly coarse linen, like sacking. For many years they had worked in their own homes, depending only on themselves for the money they made, and they did not take kindly to inter-ference in their affairs. Many times in the past there had been trouble with officials of one kind or another who had tried to tell them what they could and could

not do, and once there had been a pitched battle between the King's army on the one hand and the handloom weavers on the other. The men of Kirriemuir
would even shed their blood to maintain their independence.

But something was happening at this time which even
the handloom weavers could not fight, and as he grew
older James became aware of the rapidly increasing
shadow under which his father lived. The family often
talked of it, and one occasion he particularly remembered, although he must have been very young at the
time. Perhaps it was because of the unaccustomed
seriousness of his father's face.

'I doubt we'll not be workin' much longer, Margaret,'
he said one night when the lamps were lit and the coals
were red in the hearth and the rain splattered heavily
on the parlour window behind the curtains drawn tight
shut to keep the weather out.

Margaret looked up from the stocking she was knitting. Already James knew that her hands were never
idle, and even when she was resting from baking and
sewing and cleaning and washing and ironing and
mending she would pick up a stocking and begin
knitting.

'Whatever dae ye mean, David?' she asked.

David Barrie sat on one of the hair-bottomed chairs,
his hands clasped tightly in front of him, his eyes fixed
on the glowing coals.

'Rab Gilchrist came intae the loom shop today,' he
said. 'He's just back from Dundee.'

He was silent and a coal settled suddenly in a shower
of sparks.

'Aye?' said Margaret quietly.

'The power mills are operatin' there,' said David.

'The handloom weavin's dyin'. There's men lyin' idle
while machines dae their work.'

'A machine could never turn out as good linen as a
handloom,' declared Margaret.

David Barrie shook his head.

'I doubt they can,' he said. 'They can turn it out
faster and cheaper and mebbe even better than the
handloom.'

'Havers,' said Margaret stoutly.

'I wish it was havers, but it's not. We hae tae face the
facts. There's mills in Dundee and I hear tell there's
goin' tae be a mill at Forfar. Dundee's not twenty
miles away. It'll not be long before there's a mill here
at Kirriemuir.'

James could not understand exactly what his father
meant, but there were many references to this mill
which seemed to worry Mr Barrie. What a mill was he
had no idea, but he gradually formed a picture in his
mind of some Giant who would steal away his father's
handloom on which they all depended for their living,
and he knew with a little thrill of fear that this Giant
was rapidly approaching Kirriemuir and might arrive
at any time.

One of the first things James had clear memories of
was going to the Kirk on Sundays. Margaret Ogilvy –
she was always known, after the old Scots fashion, by
her maiden name – had been a member of a very strict
church called the Auld Licht, or Old Light, Church,
but when she married David Barrie she joined his
church. There were many different churches in Kirriemuir, most of them very small like the Auld Lichts, and
the Barries now attended the South Free Church.

How James remembered those endless Sundays in

the cold, bare dismal church where there was neither
organ nor harmonium – a 'kist of whistles', the congregation would contemptuously call such things – and
the psalms were read out by the minister line by line
and the precentor gave the congregation the key by
singing the line before everyone took it up! How he
remembered the endless sermons delivered from the
pulpit! The congregation were well satisfied with their
minister, for he never had a written sermon, not even
a page of notes. He would stare sternly from the pulpit
at the congregation, clear his throat importantly, start
his sermon and go on and on and on, and though
James never had any idea what he was talking about,
he could not help admiring a man who could talk
straight off for an hour and a half or two hours and
never stumble or stutter. He could admire it, but that
did not stop him from fidgetting uncomfortably in his
hard pew and wishing he could look out of the high
window to see what was happening in the brighter
world outside. On these occasions he felt rather like a
prisoner.

Sometimes the results of these Sunday services were
rather startling. When the family returned home to the
Tenements, Margaret would turn suddenly to Jane Ann.

'Jane Ann, off with that Sunday dress of yours. I
want it!'

'What for, Mother?' Jane Ann would say.

'Did ye not see the banker's daughter in the kirk this
morning?'

'Aye. I noticed her.'

'And did ye not notice the dress she was wearing?'

'Aye, but –'

'Those new puffy sleeves . . . If I were tae take a
panel out of that old lilac petticoat of mine I could put

sleeves like that intae your dress for next Sunday. Then
ye'll be in the height of fashion too!'

And Jane Ann would have to go and change into her
everyday dress and give her mother her Sunday best,
and Margaret would get busy with scissors and needle
and thread, and as if by magic the new sleeves would
appear on the old dress, and it would look like something out of the latest fashion magazines and no one
would ever guess that the same sort of changes had
been made to the dress at least ten times before.

James himself always wore clothes handed down from
his brothers. Clothes that Alexander had worn many
years before had been passed on to David and then,
with slight alterations, to him, but so cunning was
Margaret with her needle and thread that his clothes
looked as if they were brand new, even the knicker-
bockers that David had been sliding down the brae in
not very long before.

Margaret Ogilvy was amazing. She only had to see
one of the ladies of quality in the street or catch a
glimpse of one as she slipped into her pew in church,
and she had a clear picture in her mind of everything
she wore. Within a matter of hours she could convert an
old dress or hat into something very similar to the
original which might have cost ten shillings or more.

There was only one article of the children's clothing
which she had not made, and that was the delicate white
robe in which every Barrie child had been christened,
from Alexander right down to little Margaret, and in-
cluding the two girls who had died so young. James had
worn it on the Sunday after he was born when he was
christened in the South Free Church. She kept it
wrapped in a wooden chest and occasionally removed it
to shake out non-existent dust and smooth out the

creases, and sometimes the robe was lent to a neighbour or a friend for the christening of one of their children, and when the child was presented in the church, Margaret would nudge whichever of her own children sat next to her and whisper:

'Does the bairn not look bonny in our wee dress?'

She had bought it in a fit of extravagance for Alexander's christening because, she said, she wanted one thing which came from a shop and which she had not made herself.

Alexander was something of a mystery to James. It seemed impossible that this big, cheerful man with the booming laugh could be his brother, for Alexander was eighteen when James was born and was studying to be a teacher at Aberdeen University, so he was at home only during the holidays. James was in awe of Alexander who always seemed closer in age to his father than to himself.

By the time James was old enough to take notice Alexander had taken his degree and had opened a school of his own at Bothwell in Lanarkshire, and James's oldest sister Mary went there to help him run it. Whenever they came home during the holidays there was always great activity in the house. Margaret would spend the day before their arrival baking, and James would watch round-eyed as batch after batch of bannocks and scones was taken from the oven, each of them perfectly baked, golden and glowing and never one of them broken. The family was very proud of Alexander, but Margaret always felt that he could not possibly be properly looked after in Bothwell and needed plenty of good food whenever he came home.

She respected Alexander but she loved David. David, the middle son, always tousle-headed and harum-scarum, usually with a cut on his knee or the seat torn out of his trousers after a game of football in the yard or from climbing trees. David, the one who, to James's great envy, could actually *whistle*, a feat which he had not yet learnt himself. Margaret loved all her children, but she loved David best.

Jane Ann seemed like a second mother to James. Now that Mary was away with Alexander it was she who was always helping about the house, cleaning, laying fires, carrying coals and water, doing the hundred and one jobs which Margaret could never have tackled on her own. Often it was Jane Ann who would comfort him if he fell down on the cobbles in the yard and hurt himself, and it was Jane Ann who might fetch needle and thread to patch up some article of clothing which had got torn.

Sometimes James would go to the loom shop where his father did his weaving now. The big loom with its wide wheel to one side, and the clatter of the shuttle as it flashed backwards and forwards carrying the weft across the warp and back again seemed to fascinate him, and he loved to watch his father, his face intent on the job, the skill of the craftsman in his hands as he mended broken threads with the thrums, or lengths of linen thread which hung at the back of the loom for the purpose. As he watched the care and love which his father used in his work James sometimes thought of that mysterious Giant who was coming to Kirriemuir to take his father's livelihood away, but when he mentioned it his father only laughed.

'Never you heed about the mill, my laddie,' Mr Barrie would say. 'It'll not bother you. You'll not be a handloom weaver, and nor will your brothers. I'm the last of them, and that's a fact. The last of a long line, and it's sad that that should be so, but ye canna stop progress. There'll be better things for you, you'll see.'

Mr Barrie was not an educated man. He had never had much schooling, but as a sober, God-fearing, thoughtful Scots craftsman he had taught himself to read the Bible and would spend his evenings reading the good book, picking out the words one by one with a large forefinger, his lips moving to form the sound, and like most of his kind he had a tremendous respect for learning. That was why he had saved to put his oldest boy through the University of Aberdeen, and why he was hoping that the coming of the power loom would not prevent him from doing the same for his other sons as well.

And here Alexander was soon able to help. After he had settled into his school at Bothwell Alexander decided that young David should have the chance of an education too, and he offered to take David into his school. He would receive a good education which would not cost a lot of money his parents could ill afford, and he would live with Alexander and Mary in the house they had set up.

And so when James was barely six years old the whole family trooped down to the station one day to see a flushed and excited David on to the train. He had only to change at Forfar and Alexander would meet him at the other end. David was bubbling over at the adventure, but Margaret found it difficult to hold back her tears.

'Now be a good laddie, David,' she said as David leant out of the carriage window to say his last goodbyes. 'And dae what your brother Alexander tells ye. Now, mind.'

'Dinna you fret, Mother. I'll be fine,' said David.

He kissed Jane Ann and Isabella and Sara and chucked baby Margaret under the chin, shook hands solemnly with his father, and then clapped James on the shoulder.

'You'll hae tae look after the old folk now, Jamie,' he said with a grin. 'I dinna ken how ye'll manage for they're an awful handful to wrestle with!'

'Och, David!' said Margaret with something between a hiccup and a laugh.

At the end of the train the guard blew his whistle and waved his green flag.

'Mind and write and tell us how ye're gettin' on,' said Margaret as there was a whistle from the engine and the train shuddered.

David nodded and said something but his words were drowned by the hiss of steam. The train began to move.

'And mind and dae your lessons right and dinna be disgracin' your brother and him an important teacher,' called Margaret.

David nodded again and began to wave as the train slowly gathered speed. James thought he saw him swallow and blink back a tear though that did not seem at all like David, and in the steam from the train he could not be sure.

They stood on the platform and waved until the train had disappeared round a bend.

'Eh, dear,' said Margaret. 'I hope he'll be all right. I never did trust these new-fangled railways. Jane Ann, will ye take wee Margaret a minute. I doubt – I doubt I must hae got a smut in my eye.'

As she wiped her eyes with her hanky to get rid of the non-existent smut they heard the train whistle in the distance, but they could no longer see it as it rattled busily along the single track to Forfar, carrying David on the first stage of his long journey.

They could not know it, but they would never see him again.

3

David

It was a cold, crisp, clear day near the end of January when the message came. Although he was only six years old it was a day James would never forget, because this was the day when his whole life changed.

It had snowed during the night and the yard outside the house was clean and white, dimpled here and there with the footsteps of people who had crossed from their houses to the washhouse on the far side. The sky had cleared and the frost made the whole countryside look as sharp as a needle. Smoke curled lazily from house chimneys into the still air, smudging the pale blue of the sky with grey, and everything seemed very quiet.

Isabella and Sara and James were trying to teach three-year-old Margaret how to make a snowball and roll it across the snow so that it grew bigger and bigger and eventually became the body of a snowman. Inside the house they could hear their mother and Jane Ann chatting together as they went about the task of cleaning the house and preparing the midday meal.

They were at the far side of the yard, intent on their snowball, and the telegraph boy's footsteps must have been muffled in the soft snow, for they did not hear anything until he knocked on the door. Then they stopped work on the snowball and stared in surprise at the blue uniform and the pill-box hat, for they had never seen a telegraph boy in the Tenements before.

They ran to the door. Just as they reached it it opened and Margaret Ogilvy stood there.

'Telegram for Barrie,' said the telegraph boy. He thrust the thin envelope into Margaret's hand and turned and left the yard. James heard him whistling as he went.

Margaret stood quite still and her face drained of colour. She looked down at the envelope with fear in her eyes.

Jane Ann suddenly appeared behind her.

'What is it, Mother?' she asked.

Margaret slowly looked round at her.

'A telegram,' she said so quietly that James could hardly hear her. 'It – it must be bad news.'

'What does it say?' asked Jane Ann.

Margaret handed her the unopened envelope.

Jane Ann took it and slit it open. The rustle of the tearing paper seemed very loud in the quiet yard. She opened out the form inside and looked at it. For a moment she did not move, and then she clutched her mother's arm and looked across at James.

'Jamie, fetch Father from the loom,' she said.

'But we're makin' a snowman,' protested James.

'Fetch Father!' said Jane Ann, and the tone of her voice sent James running for the loom shop without any further argument.

In two minutes, panting and breathless, he was back in the yard with his father beside him. The yard was empty now, the half-completed snowman's body lying abandoned in the far corner.

They rushed into the house and found the family crowded into the parlour, the girls all unnaturally silent and solemn-looking.

'What's the matter?' demanded Mr Barrie.

Jane Ann left the chair where her mother was sitting and handed him the telegraph form. Mr Barrie took it and read it slowly and haltingly aloud.

'*David has had accident. Important you come immediately,*' he read.

Margaret sat pale and tense in the chair. To James it looked as if she had shrunk since he had last seen her about five minutes before. She seemed to have got smaller, and her clothes seemed too big, and whereas before he had thought of her as always knowing exactly what to do and how, now she seemed lost and frightened.

'We must go tae him, David,' she said. 'We must go quickly. Alexander would never hae sent a telegram if it wasna serious.'

Mr Barrie tucked the telegraph form into his waist-coat pocket. His face was set and troubled.

B

'Aye,' he said. 'There's a train in half an hour. Jane Ann, get your mother's bonnet and shawl and her boots. Then go tae Bell Lunan's and ask if you and the bairns can bide with her till your mother and I get back.'

'Can we not come too, Father?' asked James.

Mr Barrie did not even look at him.

'No,' he said. 'Stay here with your sisters.'

He stood over his wife and looked down at her with such a strange look of pity and fear on his face that even James, who was not really sure what was happening, realised that whatever it was was very serious.

'Are ye all right, Margaret?' he asked quietly.

For a moment she did not seem to have heard him, and then she looked up, but the smile which usually came to her face was not there, and she scarcely seemed to see him.

'I'm all right, David,' she said at last, 'but we must hurry.'

Jane Ann came rushing into the room with her mother's bonnet and shawl and helped her into them. Margaret hardly seemed to know what she was doing, but in a few minutes she and Mr Barrie were dressed for outdoors and setting off for the station.

The children watched them turn into Lilybank between their house and Bell Lunan's. Neither of their parents looked back, and Jane Ann led a very subdued family across the yard to Bell's house, but while she was not looking James slipped away, darted through Lilybank and on to the Brechin Road and followed his father and mother towards the station. Mr Barrie had taken Margaret's arm and was guiding her, and James saw her stumble once or twice, but his father's strong hand held her and her back was very straight. The road was empty, the piercing cold and the heavy snow keeping most people indoors beside their fires. James cautiously closed the distance between him and his parents, scared that if his father saw him he might order him back, but neither of them seemed to notice him.

It made him feel a little lonely, as though they had gone away and left him, even though they were there in front of him. There was not even the usual noise of the streets to intrude on him, for the snow had blanketed all sound and it was as if the whole world were holding its breath.

He began to wish he had stayed with the others and gone to Bell Lunan's house where he could enjoy the games he often played there, hiding Bell's stick and trying to make her guess where he had put it. But something told him that games of that sort would not be enjoyed today.

The train was at the station and James followed his parents on to the platform. Mr Barrie caught sight of him and James was afraid he was going to be sent home, but surprisingly Mr Barrie seemed to accept the fact that he was there without question.

'Stay with your mother, Jamie,' he said. 'I'll be back in a minute.'

James watched as his father walked quickly away towards the telegraph office and then glanced timidly at his mother. She was standing absolutely still as though she were frozen, and James shivered. It was almost as though she had become a stranger. Her eyes followed his father to the telegraph office and when the door had closed behind him her hand came out towards James and he took it gratefully. He was surprised to feel how cold it was, even through her glove.

Around them passengers were assembling to join the train, some of them calling a cheerful greeting to Mar-

garet who did not seem to hear them. Porters pushed
trolleys of luggage towards the guard's van, and everything around them seemed normal and ordinary.

A minute later the telegraph office door opened and
Mr Barrie reappeared. James could see he had a slip of
paper in his hand. His father came towards them, his
legs curiously stiff and his face set in a mask. He stopped
in front of them and for a few seconds tried to speak,
but no sound came. James felt Margaret's hand tighten
so hard in his that he nearly cried out with the pain.

At last his father spoke.

'He's gone,' he said, and his voice was little more than
a croak.

Margaret gave a strangled cry and James felt her hand
go limp in his. She swayed slightly and then her legs
seemed to fold under her and she fell to the platform
in a dead faint.

*

They brought David home and then took him sorrow-
fully from the house in the Tenements to the Hill
Cemetery a little to the north of the town and buried
him beside the other two Barrie children who had died
very young.

But this was different from the earlier deaths. The
two little girls had lived hardly more than a few months,
so although there was grief when they were taken away,
it was nothing compared with the death of David who
had been one of them for so long and who died the day
before his fourteenth birthday.

A shocked and grief-stricken Alexander told how it
had happened. He told his father alone first of all, for
Margaret was so struck down that she could scarcely
speak.

David and a friend had gone to spend the morning
skating on the frozen pond near Alexander's house in
Bothwell. They only had one pair of skates between
them, a present for his birthday the following day from
Alexander. David had had first shot and then come to
the edge of the pond to change and let his friend have
a turn. His friend put on the skates and then, as he got
up he slipped and cannoned into David. David fell and
hit his head on the ice. He died shortly after they had
carried him back to Alexander's house.

Margaret did not attend the funeral service on the
cold, bleak hillside. She lay on her bed with the curtains
drawn, never moving, hardly eating, and the ever-
faithful Jane Ann stayed with her, watching over her
day and night.

The doctor came and went several times, and he
shook his head worriedly. There seemed nothing he
could do.

Days passed. The house seemed sunk in an unnatural
silence. Where there had been laughter and happy
chatter before there was now furtive whispering and
tiptoeing from room to room. Mr Barrie, silent and lost-
looking, went back to his loom, for the weaving still had
to be done to support the family. Alexander returned
to Bothwell. The younger children, frightened and not
understanding what had happened, were quiet, because
the one of them who had made most noise in the house
with his cheerful whistling and his laughter would
never whistle or laugh again.

*

James sat on the stairs which led up to his mother's
room. He had taken to sitting here, thinking that he

might be the first to see her when she eventually re-appeared and came back to cook the meals and start life all over again.

So far she had not come. He had looked in through the door of her room several times, but the darkness and the silence had frightened him.

Now it was a week after the funeral. The snow had gone and the yard was swept by gusts of sleety rain and he could hear the wind howling mournfully round the chimney pots.

He heard the latch of his mother's door click and he turned round, his heart thumping eagerly, thinking it might be her at last.

But it was only Jane Ann.

She came down the stairs and he squeezed himself into one wall, making himself as small as possible to give her room to pass, but instead of passing she stopped and sat down on the stair beside him.

He looked at her in surprise but said nothing, and for a time they were silent. Looking at her it seemed as if Jane Ann had suddenly become very much older, though she was not yet twenty.

'You're the only one who can help her, Jamie,' she said at last.

'Me, Jane Ann?'

'Aye. I've tried. And Father's tried. And the doctor's tried. And no one can dae anything with her.'

'But what can I dae?'

'I'm not quite sure.'

There was silence again, and in the silence James heard the creak of the bed upstairs and something between a sigh and a moan filtered through the closed door of his mother's room.

Jane Ann started up and stood on the stair listening,

waiting to hear if her mother should call to her, but the silence had fallen again and after a minute Jane Ann sat down again beside her brother.

'She's grievin' sore for him, Jamie,' she said. 'We must dae something.'

'Aye, but what?'

'If she goes on this way she may die, Jamie.'

James stared at her in sudden fear. The thought of his mother dying was one that had never struck him, and it filled him with horror. That couldn't happen!

'No!' he cried. 'She canna!'

'She may,' said Jane Ann. Suddenly she gripped his arm tightly. 'Go tae her, Jamie,' she whispered tensely. 'Go in tae her.'

He stared at her round-eyed, his heart pounding uncomfortably.

'But – but she'll not speak. What'll I say?'

'Tell her – tell her she's got another son!'

James looked into his sister's eyes. It seemed a strange thing to be told to say. His mother knew she had another son. Two, in fact. Alexander and himself.

'She can only think of – of David just now,' said Jane Ann. 'And the thought of him lyin' up there in the cemetery is like tae drive her mad. Tell her she's got another son tae think of!'

James had never heard his sister speak like that before, and without quite realising he was doing it he got slowly to his feet and began to climb the stairs. At the top he hesitated and looked down. Jane Ann was standing looking up at him, and she smiled encouragingly at him and nodded.

James gulped slightly, lifted the latch and squeezed into the room.

It was dark, with the curtains drawn across the small

window, and it took a little while for his eyes to grow accustomed to the gloom. Then he began to make out the shadowy shapes of the furniture, the dresser and the chair and the bed. It seemed awfully quiet and for a horrible moment he wondered if Jane Ann was right, if his mother had died and for some reason she had not told him.

He could see her lying quite still on the bed, and he saw something white lying on the pillow beside her. After a moment he realised what it was. It was the robe in which all the children had been christened, but James knew that at that time she had only been thinking of one of them.

There was a stir of movement from the bed and a small, tired voice whispered:

'Is that you?'

James gulped and did not answer. The voice seemed so small and weak it was scarcely like his mother's at all. The silence seemed to stretch on and on and then the voice said again:

'Is that you?'

And suddenly James thought he knew what she meant. She was thinking only of David, Jane Ann had said. No one else had a place in her mind at the moment. And she thought it was David standing there in her room. He felt tears sting his eyes as he suddenly blurted out:

'No, it's not him. It's only me.'

There was a sudden strangled sob from the bed and in the grey light James saw his mother stir and hold out her arms. With tears streaming down his face he ran to her.

*

Margaret's recovery was very slow but it started on that day. James was shocked at the change in her when he first saw her again in daylight. The happy, cheerful face had gone, leaving a sad, empty look, and from then on his great occupation was to try to make her laugh as she had done before.

But it was not easy.

He would stand on his head at the top of the bed with his feet planted against the wall, and Margaret could hear his anxious voice, muffled because he was upside down, calling:

'Are ye laughin', Mother?'

And Margaret would smile stiffly because she knew he was trying to make her happy.

James was sure that if only he could take David's place his mother would be all right, so he set about trying to be as like David as he could. He practised for a long time, and then one day, flushed and triumphant, he ran into the kitchen and shouted:

'Mother – look!'

Margaret turned from the oven with a tray of bannocks in her hands. James stood with his legs wide apart, hands thrust into the pocket of his knicker-bockers, and after one or two unsuccessful attempts, managed to give vent to a piercing whistle. It was really a terrible noise, but he was very proud of it, for he had only just learnt how to do it.

Margaret blinked and her eyes seemed a little moist.

'Oh, my laddie,' she said at last, 'dinna try tae be like him. Just be like yourself. That's all ye need tae dae.'

He was disappointed that he had not made her laugh.

One day as the doctor was leaving after one of his visits, James caught him in the yard and with the air of one telling a great secret, showed him a crushed and crumpled piece of paper.

'What's this ye have, Jamie?' asked the doctor.

'It's my laugh record,' said James breathlessly. 'See, doctor. Every time she laughs I mark it down on the paper there.'

The doctor looked at the dirty little scrap of paper with the rows of squiggly lines on it, and he laughed aloud.

'My, Jamie, that's a good idea,' he said. 'And here, will I tell ye how tae get another laugh tae add tae your collection?'

'Aye, doctor, please.'

'Show her the paper. I'll wager that'll make her laugh.'

'Dae ye think sae?'

'I'm sure of it.'

'Then I'll try.'

The doctor laughed again and slapped him on the shoulder.

James ran into the house and found his mother and Jane Ann washing dishes in the kitchen. Carefully and breathlessly he explained to Margaret what the paper meant, and Margaret listened. He watched her anxiously. He saw the corners of her mouth tremble and then she suddenly chuckled. Delighted, James seized the paper and pulled a stump of pencil out of his pocket. He marked down another laugh very carefully. When she saw what he was doing Margaret laughed again, and James triumphantly marked down a second laugh, though really he was not quite sure whether it should count as one long one or two separate ones.

From then on Margaret became more herself, but she never again was as happy and carefree as she had been before David's death. Often a faraway look would come into her eyes, and when he saw this James hastened to talk to her, to make her think of something else.

Margaret and James grew very close to one another from this time onwards, and this closeness was something which James would never forget.

4

Stories

James went to school when he was six.

He was perhaps a little small for his age, with a gentle, rather solemn face which could suddenly light up into impish mischief. But although he did not look sturdy he was strong and wiry and his mother was quite glad of the chance to send him to a little school in the town each morning, for he was a bright boy and needed some occupation to use up his energies.

The night before he went to school for the first time Margaret spent hours ironing and mending, making sure his clothes looked neat and clean for the big adventure, while James watched all the preparations a little anxiously, not quite sure what to expect the following day.

In the morning he was scrubbed clean and his hair plastered down with water and carefully brushed, and Margaret took him by the hand and walked with him out of the Tenements and along the road to Bank Street.

She led him to a neat little house with carefully tended flower beds in its front garden and apple trees growing against the wall, and James, who had been a little worried about what he was going to find when he went to school, felt reassured at this peaceful scene.

The door was opened by a very small lady dressed in a simple dark dress with a lace cap on her head.

'Why, good morning, Mistress Barrie,' she said when she saw Margaret, and for a moment Margaret looked puzzled. She was so rarely addressed by her married name that it sounded strange to her. 'What a lovely morning it is, to be sure.'

'Aye, it's a fine day, Miss Adam,' said Margaret. 'I just brought Jamie down, seein' it's his first day at the school.'

Miss Adam looked down at James and smiled at him.

'So this is James,' she said. 'How do you do, James?'

She held out her hand to him, and for a moment James was not sure what he should do. Then very gingerly he put out his own hand and touched hers. Miss Adam clutched it in a dry, gentle grip and shook hands with him.

'I'm sure we shall get along very well together,' said Miss Adam. 'Thank you for bringing him, Mistress

Barrie. My sister and I will see that he returns to you at midday. Do you have a handkerchief with you, James?'

James nodded. His mother had put a clean one in his trousers pocket just before they left the house.

'I'll away then,' said Margaret. 'Now, be a good laddie, Jamie, and mind and dae what Miss Adam tells ye.'

She ruffled his hair, spoiling the freshly brushed look she had spent so much time on, said goodbye to Miss Adam, and made her way down the garden path to the gate.

'Come along, then, James. Let us go in,' said Miss Adam. 'Just a minute! Please wipe your feet very carefully on the mat. You must do that every time you enter the house, otherwise we might find the carpets in a dreadful mess, might we not?'

James always thought of that school as the Hanky School. Every morning when one of the Misses Adam held prayers, the pupils had to spread their hankies on the floor before they knelt down so as to prevent their dirty knees from soiling the carpet.

The Misses Adam were gentle creatures, constantly worried about the state of the furniture and the wallpaper when little hands and feet were around the house. They were the daughters of a minister who had had a church in the south of Scotland and who had retired to Kirriemuir, and although James learnt no lessons there he certainly learnt a lot about manners, for the Misses Adam made sure that all their pupils behaved like little ladies and gentlemen in the house.

James did not always take kindly to the gentility which was forced on him. Once, when the older Miss Adam was really very cross with him because he had

been fighting with another boy, he found himself locked
in the coal cellar which was under the stairs leading to
the upper part of the house where the Adam family
lived.

On another occasion he was sent out of the room in
deep disgrace for bringing some mud into the house on
his boot and leaving it on the schoolroom carpet. What
a fluttering there was with brushes and dustpans and
damp cloths to get the mark out! And James was sent
to sit on the stairs outside until the Misses Adam had
relented enough to let him in again.

He sat there quite contentedly, listening to the drone
of the children's voices as they came through the closed
door of the schoolroom. Sunlight slanted through the
glass above the front door and little specks of dust
danced gently in its rays. James wondered what the
Misses Adam would say if they could see that dust. He
could imagine them running around with dusters trying
to chase the specks of dust out of the front door, uttering
little cries of distress and alarm as they did so.

It was a funny picture, that, and he was sitting enjoying it when suddenly he heard a creak on the stair
behind him.

He turned and saw an old gentleman coming slowly
down. He was dressed in black and he had long snowy-
white hair, and James scrambled hastily to his feet. This
was the Misses Adam's father, the retired minister, and
though James had sometimes seen him from a distance
pottering around in the garden when he was in the
schoolroom he had never seen him so close before.

'Hey, hey, what's this?' said Mr Adam when he caught
sight of James standing at the foot of the stairs. 'Here's
a laddie been sent out of the classroom, eh? What's
your name, laddie, eh?'

'Please, sir, James Barrie.'

'James Barrie, eh? And why were ye sent out of the classroom, James Barrie?'

'Please, sir, I had some mud on my shoe, and I didna notice till I got inside and the mud got on the carpet and made a mess.'

'It did, eh? Well, mud's got a habit of doing that. How long have ye been out here, eh?'

'I dinna ken, sir, but it's an awful long time.'

'Tuts, tuts. That's a shame, now.'

Mr Adam began to feel in the pocket of his jacket and eventually pulled something out.

'Here, then, James Barrie. Here's something that'll mebbe help to pass the time, eh?'

And he handed James a peppermint. James thanked him and popped it into his mouth. Mr Adam patted him on the head and made his way out of the front door and down the garden path.

James sat down again, happily sucking his peppermint, and when at last the Misses Adam relented and called him back into the schoolroom the peppermint had gone. After that James was quite keen to be sent out of the room, and when that happened he would sit on the stairs and cough and make slight noises, trying to attract the attention of Mr Adam upstairs in the hope of getting another peppermint.

*

James returned home from school at midday and he would throw open the door of the house and call out:

'Are ye there, Margaret Ogilvy?'

From somewhere in the house, usually either the kitchen or the parlour, Margaret would call back:

'Yes, James Barrie. I'm here.'

And James could usually tell by the tone of her voice whether she was happy or sad.

He still made it his duty to watch over her and make sure she was kept contented and was not allowed to think too much of the son who had died. Whenever he saw that strained, faraway look come into her eyes he would think quickly of some way of distracting her.

One way he found of doing this was to get her to talk about Kirriemuir as it had been when she was a girl. Sometimes she would fall silent in the evenings and the stocking she was knitting would lie idle in her lap while her eyes turned unseeingly to the fire. If he asked her to tell him something about the people she had known in those far off days she would immediately do so and the dangerous moment would be past.

And he found these stories fascinating. She would tell him about the quaint characters of the Auld Licht Church, that strangely strict little church in which she had been brought up, and she had a way of telling the stories which brought the people vividly to life, though almost all of them were long dead, and their way of life was one which James had no knowledge of himself.

Especially she told him of her own father, Alexander Ogilvy, who had been a stonemason. His wife had died when Margaret was eight years old, and she had been left at that early age with the job of looking after the house and her father and younger brother. Her father had been a pillar of the Auld Licht Church, a man of simple faith and piety, and she loved him very dearly. She told James how in all weathers she would run from their house at midday to carry her father's dinner to him, wherever he was working, in a flagon.

'I had a pale blue dress with a blue bonnet with

white ribbons,' she said, smiling into the fire and seeing herself as she had been nearly forty years before.

'Ye must hae looked very pretty, Mother,' said James.

She smiled at him a little shyly.

'I wouldna say that,' she said. 'But blue was aye my colour.'

Her father died long before James was born, but he knew her brother, David Ogilvy who was a minister with a church in Motherwell.

James treasured these stories, not only because in telling them Margaret was returning to her own youth and forgetting the more recent tragedy, but because he himself began to picture these people his mother spoke of, people he had never met, but who became as real to him as his school friends.

*

He did not stay long at the Hanky School. Very soon he was moved to the South Free Church School, a school attached to the church where the family worshipped, and here began his real education. He discovered the joys of reading and writing, and the somewhat lesser joys of arithmetic.

Reading opened up vast new ideas. Soon after he had learnt to read he ordered a halfpenny magazine which came out once a month, and he would count the days to the appearance of the next number. On the day it came he would rush away with it into a corner and devour the serial stories, losing himself in a melodramatic land of pirates and robbers, ladies in distress, knights in armour and all kinds of things, until Jane Ann's voice broke in on his dreams to call him to a meal.

One month the magazine was late in coming. He

went to Mills's newspaper shop in Bank Street, near the old Hanky School, full of eagerness, and found to his intense disappointment that the magazine had not arrived. Feeling strangely empty he walked home again, and found his mother in the parlour making a clooty rug from some old rags she had found in her sewing box.

James poured out his tale of woe.

'Well, Jamie,' said Margaret, stitching away busily, 'ye'll just hae tae wait till your magazine comes in. It'll not be more than a day or two.'

'A day or two!' said James in horror. That was a lifetime when you were waiting for the next episode of a thrilling serial story. 'I – I canna wait that long, Mother!'

'I doubt ye must.'

'But I want tae ken what happens! I want to ken if the pirates really make Lady Cynthia walk the plank. There's sharks in the water and she'll get eaten if she does. I've got tae ken!'

But Margaret could not help him. He wandered restlessly round the room, and eventually went and sat down beside her.

'Tell me again about the lady who walked out of the Auld Licht Church whenever they started singing a psalm, Mother,' he said. He had heard the story before, but perhaps hearing it again might help to pass the time and make him forget about the terrible problem of what was going to happen to Lady Cynthia.

Margaret sighed.

'I canna just now, Jamie,' she said. 'I've got this rug tae finish and I canna concentrate on it while I'm tellin' stories.'

James's face fell and he stared gloomily into the fire

for a while. Margaret glanced at him and then an idea struck her.

'I ken what ye should dae,' she said. 'If ye're all that anxious tae ken what happened tae Lady – what was her name – ?'

'Cynthia.'

'That's an odd name. It'll be English, I suppose. Well, if ye want tae ken what happened tae Lady Cynthia, why dae ye not make it up yourself?'

'Make it up?'

'Aye. Find yourself some paper and a pencil and write what ye think happened tae her. Then when the magazine comes ye can find out if ye've thought of the same thing as the man that writes the story.'

James stared at her open-mouthed. How clever she was! It was so simple, so obvious, and yet he had never thought of it himself! Why shouldn't he write the story himself?

Filled with a sudden enthusiasm he clattered away to find paper and pencil to begin the task of rescuing Lady Cynthia from the pirates. Margaret smiled as he dashed out of the room. At least she would now be able to finish her rug in peace.

But she was wrong.

At the end of every hastily scribbled page James came tearing down the stairs to read what he had written to her, his face flushed with pride, as he stumbled breathlessly over the words. Margaret had to admire his efforts and make suggestions and criticisms until she felt it would perhaps have been easier just to tell him the story of the lady who walked out of the Auld Licht Church every time the congregation sang a psalm.

From then on James often scribbled stories of his own, all in the style of his favourite magazine, full of bold deeds and wonderful adventures, of brave men and beautiful heroines. He would read these stories to his friends during the breaks at school, and they would gasp with wonder and wait as eagerly for the next instalment of a story as he himself had waited for the arrival of each new edition of his magazine.

His mother, too, would listen to his stories and when he had finished reading them to her she would ask him questions about the people in them and they would talk about them and discuss them as though they were real people.

'Dae ye think they're good, Mother?' James asked, anxious for her praise.

'Very good, Jamie,' she replied, because she knew that would please him. 'Maybe ye'll be a writer when ye grow up.'

James was silent for so long that Margaret glanced down at him where he sat on the floor beside her, wondering if she had said the wrong thing. He was staring out of the window with a faraway look on his face.

'What is it, Jamie?' she asked gently.

He was silent for a long time.

'I dinna want tae grow up,' he said at last.

Margaret was surprised.

'Ye dinna want tae grow up?' she echoed. 'I thought all lads and lassies couldna wait tae grow up.'

'Well, I dinna!'

'Why not?'

'I dinna want tae give up playing games and enjoying myself. I dinna want tae become old and slow and – and sad. I want tae stay just as I am and be with you, Mother.'

He looked at her with such a mournful expression on

his face that she found it difficult not to smile, but at the same time she felt tears sting her eyes. She knew better than he that what worried him most was the thought that when he grew up he would no longer be able to lose himself in fine imaginary stories of pirates and robbers and Jacobites being hunted through the glens by redcoat soldiers. He would have to become sober and matter-of-fact – in short, he would have to *be* grown up.

'Well, d'ye ken, Jamie, I never wanted tae grow up either,' she said, 'sae we must be very much the same, you and me.'

'And how did ye feel when ye *did* grow up, Mother?'

'I didna notice much difference, tae tell ye the truth, Jamie. It's not sae bad as ye seem tae think it is. I can promise ye that.'

But James was not convinced. The thought of any change in his life upset him. Although he knew in his heart that it was impossible, he wanted to stay the same as he was now.

Besides his own stories he and Margaret used to read books together. They enjoyed *The Pilgrim's Progress,* but perhaps their favourite was *Robinson Crusoe.* They marvelled at Crusoe's adventures on his desert island and never failed to be thrilled at his discovery of the naked footprint in the sand, and James was fascinated to know that the real man on whom Robinson Crusoe was based was a Scotsman, Alexander Selkirk, who had lived not far to the south in the little Fife fishing village of Largo.

These times with his mother were precious to him and he was to remember them all his life.

*

James spent a lot of his time in W. B. Mills's newspaper shop in Bank Street. Apart from newspapers there were books and magazines here, and James would spend hours browsing through them.

Mr Mills was a kindly man who allowed James to look through the papers and magazines as much as he liked. He knew the lad could not afford to buy them, the one magazine every month which cost a halfpenny being all that James could afford, but Mr Mills never discouraged him from reading anything which stood on the counter of the little shop. Mr Mills had a son who went to the same school as James, and one day the boy saw James in the shop and called him through to the back premises. James slipped through the curtain and followed young Mills up the stairs to the room above the shop. It was a living room with a window looking out over the street, a few tables and chairs and in one wall a concealed bed hidden from view during the day by curtains drawn across it.

Standing on a table in the middle of the room was a square boxlike thing, and young Mills showed it to James.

'What is it?' asked James, puzzled.

'It's a toy theatre.'

'A theatre? How does it work?'

Young Mills began to explain the theatre to James. He showed him the curtains which came down over the opening in the front, and the gaily coloured back cloths which could be slipped into place to form the scenery.

'But what does it do?' asked James.

'Ye make plays with it.'

'Plays?'

'Aye. See. Here are the people who act in the theatre.'

From a small box young Mills produced a selection
of stiff cardboard figures. There was a bearded man in
armour with one arm raised carrying a sword. There
was a woman with a shawl over her head and her hands
held out as though she were pleading with someone.
There was a child carrying a little wooden bowl, and
an old man with long white hair wearing what looked
like a nightgown, and many others. Each figure had a
length of wire attached to it, leading out from the side.

'What dae ye dae with them?' asked James. The
figures fascinated him with their gay colouring and
brightly painted faces.

'Ye make them act. Look. I'll show ye.'

Young Mills lowered the curtain in front of the
stage and got ready a back cloth. Then he picked up
two of the cardboard figures and pushed them on to
the stage. Carefully he guided James round in front of
the theatre so that he was looking directly at the
crimson-painted curtains.

'Sit there and watch,' he said.

Wondering, James sat while his friend busied himself with mysterious tasks at the back of the theatre.
Then suddenly the curtain rose and James found himself looking at a miniature scene. The back cloth
showed tall stone pillars, a blue sky and coloured bushes
at the sides, and in front of this stood two of the cardboard figures, the woman who seemed to be pleading
and the bearded man with the raised sword. The light
from the window fell directly on the scene.

The whole thing seemed almost magically real. Then
the figures moved jerkily as young Mills twitched the
wires to which they were attached, and James heard his
friend's voice, gruff and deep when he was speaking

for the man and high pitched and shrill when he was speaking for the woman.

Gruffly: 'Give me your jools or I'll murder ye!'

Shrilly: 'Oh, please dinna murder me. Think of all my bairns!'

'Give me your jools then!'

'Oh, take my jools but spare my life!'

The woman's figure moved jerkily towards the man.

'Ah-ha! These jools is worth a king's ran-sum. Ho! Ho! Ho!'

'Oh, my jools! My jools!'

The female figure collapsed on the stage and the bearded man moved slowly off and out of sight behind the pillar of the little theatre.

James sat entranced. For the first time in his life he had seen something acted on a stage, and though the cardboard figures never looked real and the voices had been almost comical, there had been a magic in the experience which he had never known before.

'That's wonderful!' he breathed. 'Ye could make real scenes for Lady Cynthia and the pirates and have all sorts of things happening.'

'Aye. It's fun. My father got it in the shop the other day and he gave it tae me.'

'Could I play with it sometimes?'

'Of course. That's what it's for. We could make up plays and think about what the people hae tae say –'

'And paint special things for the scenery –'

'And make different people for different parts –'

'And ye could put the theatre on the bed there and hide behind the curtains so no one would ken ye were there. And then it would be really real –'

'And we could get our friends in and charge them tae see a play –'

'And – and – Oh, here, it'll be *great!*'

James played often with the toy theatre above Mills's shop in Bank Street. The front of the theatre stood at the edge of the bed with the bed curtains draped round it, so that their friends could sit on the floor of the room and watch what happened on the tiny stage. They made up little scenes for the cardboard figures to speak, and lying there in the stuffy darkness behind the curtains, moving the little figures and speaking in funny voices, James discovered a whole new world he had never known before, a world of magic and make-believe which he was never to forget.

5

Games

The Bailie strutted along the Kirk Wynd. His top hat
was brushed smooth and his coat with the fur collar was
immaculate. He looked very full of his own importance.
He had been at a meeting of the Town Council and felt
he had shown up very well there. On one occasion during the meeting he had even managed to put the Provost
in his place – very politely, of course, because it would
never do to make an enemy of the Provost – and as

he remembered it he felt his chest swell with pride.

He looked round the narrow street he was in and nodded to himself. Kirriemuir was a bonny place, he thought, a thriving place, and he was a very important man in Kirriemuir. Really, life was very good. He took a deep breath of the cool evening air and let it ruffle his big side-whiskers as he let it out again.

It was the gloaming, the time when it was neither day nor night. You could see your way, because overhead the sky was still fairly bright, but between the houses in the street the shadows were growing and the close mouths and the small square windows and doors were becoming more difficult to make out. Night was coming fast, and lights were beginning to glow in the windows. Through them he could see the good folk of Kirriemuir going about their evening duties.

The Bailie was on his way home to supper, and there he would tell his wife of the Town Council meeting and how he had made a good impression there. That would please her. She had a tremendous respect for him and he would enjoy hearing her little gasps of admiration and cries of delight as he told her just how clever he had been.

Ahead of him he caught sight of something lying in the gutter at the edge of the road, and he frowned in annoyance. Rubbish lying out in the road for important people like him to trip over! He made a mental note to bring this matter up at the next Council meeting.

As he drew near it, however, he began to doubt if it was rubbish. In the last of the fading light he could see that what was lying there was a parcel, neatly wrapped and tied with string. He bent over – not without difficulty, for he was a rather large man – and examined it. Yes, it certainly looked like a parcel. Possibly someone had dropped it without realising they had done so, though that seemed unlikely. It was very large, really, and it would be difficult to drop without knowing about it. How very careless!

But it looked an important parcel . . .

He straightened up with a grunt and looked cautiously up and down the street. It was very quiet and there was no one in sight. Certainly the parcel should not be left lying in the street where any dishonest scoundrel could pick it up and make off with it.

The Bailie was curious. It *did* look important . . .

There would be no harm, he thought, in taking it home with him. Perhaps he might even risk taking a look inside to see what it contained. If it was valuable he could hand it in to the police station the next day. Pictures of the grateful owner pouring out his thanks to him in front of a large crowd of Kirriemarians filled his mind, and he nodded to himself, already preparing the little speech he would make to the owner as he handed the parcel over. He would be pleasant, of course, but he would make it quite clear that he thought the owner was very careless to lose his parcel in the street.

He picked it up, surprised at how light it was, and with another rather guilty look up and down the street to make sure no one had seen him he tucked it under his arm and set off again in the direction of home.

He had hardly taken half a dozen steps when the parcel suddenly jerked from under his arm and fell to the ground.

The Bailie gasped and turned, looking down at the parcel in astonishment. Now how had that happened?

His eyes widened as he watched the parcel lying at his feet suddenly begin to jerk and move away from him, almost as though it were running on tiny invisible feet along the road down which he had just come. He could hear the rustle as it scraped along the ground.

The Bailie felt the hairs prickle at the back of his neck. With a hoarse cry he turned tail and, holding his top hat firmly by one hand, set off at a speed he would not have believed possible, intent on reaching the safety and comfort of his home.

Had he looked back he would have seen the parcel turn a corner into a close mouth, and had he been a little braver than he was he might have followed it and seen two small boys pulling the parcel towards them by a length of dark string.

The parcel safely recovered, the boys turned and ran through the end of the close, through a woodyard and over fences, across gardens, sure-footed in the almost vanished light, until at last, panting and breathless they reached the shelter of the washhouse in the yard behind the Tenements, where they locked themselves in and collapsed with laughter on the stone floor.

'Did ye see him?' stuttered James Barrie at last, wiping his eyes on his sleeve. 'Did ye see him? He was terrified!'

'Aye,' said the other. 'Man, that was a great idea of yours, Jamie.'

James sat up and lit a stump of candle which he set on the floor between them. He pulled the parcel towards him and began to separate the dark string from the white string which held the paper together.

'I must get this undone,' he said. 'It's my fishin' line and I'll be needin' it.'

'But we'll dae that again, will we not, Jamie?'

'Aye, Jimmy, but not too often. Otherwise folk'll begin tae get suspicious.'

Jimmy Robb nodded.

'Aye, of course,' he said. 'Man, did ye hear him howl? I've never heard the like!'

'And run! I'll bet he beat the train tae Forfar!'

And suddenly the two boys were once again rolling round the floor, helpless with laughter, until James pulled himself together and sat up.

'We're makin' too much noise,' he said. 'My mother'll hear us and come out tae see what's goin' on.'

They composed themselves once more, though every now and then a stifled giggle burst from one or the other.

James untied the last knot, carefully wound the line up and stowed it on a shelf, and then unwrapped the paper round the parcel and pulled out a few old rags and torn up pieces of paper.

'Are ye goin' fishin' in the Prosen tomorrow?' asked Jimmy.

'Aye. Mebbe.'

'What dae ye mean?'

'I've got an idea.'

Jimmy Robb fell silent. He was the younger of the two, but he knew James when he got ideas, and he was quite content to wait until the older boy had thought it out and told him what it was. James glanced thoughtfully round the washhouse. It was a tiny place with rough whitewashed walls and a big boiler in one corner where the wives in the Tenements washed the family clothes. The washhouse was filled with all sorts of odds and ends which had found their way there from the Tenements.

'I'm gettin' tired of that toy theatre,' said James at last.

'Oh?'

'Aye. Those cardboard actors arena much good. I think we could dae better.'

'How?'

'Put on a play of our own.'

'Eh? How could ye dae that?'

'Make it up, same as we dae with the toy theatre, only in this one we'd be the actors ourselves'

Jimmy Robb thought about this. It was a good idea. He had been asked some time before to help at the Mills's house with presenting plays for the toy theatre, but he knew as well as James that this ploy was beginning to lose interest. Fewer and fewer of their friends came to see the plays, and those that did were getting more and more inclined to make rude remarks about what they saw. It would be fun to be a real actor yourself, but an immediate difficulty presented itself to him.

'That would be great, Jamie, but where would we dae it? Ye'd need a stage tae act the play on and there'd hae tae be somewhere for the folk tae sit and watch.'

'That's all right,' said James. 'I've thought of that. We could dae it in here.'

'Here?' Jimmy Robb looked dubiously round the tiny washhouse.

'Aye, why not? The top of the boiler could be the stage and the audience could sit where we're sittin' now – on the floor.'

Gradually Jimmy Robb began to see possibilities.

'Aye, it could be done,' he said slowly.

'Let's you and me get up a play,' said James. 'Just us two. Then we can charge our friends tae come in and see it. I'll bet they'd come and see a real live play done by real live actors instead of those old cardboard things that always look the same.'

Jimmy Robb began to be infected by his enthusiasm.

'We could dae a pirate play,' he said. 'And the boiler could be the deck of the ship – '

'And we could put a plank up and make people walk it – '

They settled down to discuss all that they might do, the incident of the parcel and the frightened Bailie already forgotten, until they were startled by the arrival of Jane Ann who came to take James off to bed.

*

The play was accounted a great success, though not quite in the way that the two Jameses had intended.

It was a Saturday afternoon when the performance took place, a time when no one in the Tenements was likely to need the washhouse for its correct purpose, and James and Jimmy Robb were out early, waiting for the audience to turn up.

They had spread the news around school the previous day that a play was to be performed, a proper play with proper actors and none of your toy theatre stuff, and that payment for admission would be very cheap. Just 'preens, a bool or a peerie' – pins, a marble or a spinning top. They stood in the yard awaiting their audience, experiencing for the first time that peculiar sinking feeling in the pit of the stomach which actors always get before a first night. They were dressed in their best clothes with their Glengarry bonnets on, and already they were shivering with excitement.

The audience began to arrive. Each boy or girl handed over the price of admission, and soon the little cardboard box for the 'takings' was full of a motley assortment of glass marbles of different sizes, pins and one or two little wooden tops, some of them not exactly in the best of condition. The audience crowded into the washhouse and found themselves room to sit on the floor, not without a lot of pushing and squabbling, and when it seemed that no more were going to arrive, James and Jimmy Robb hid the cardboard box carefully away and went into the washhouse to start the play.

Now the trouble was that neither of them really knew what the other was going to do. They had not written down what they were going to say, and although they knew vaguely the story they were going to try to act they suddenly found it was very difficult to act it without knowing exactly what was going to happen. It was all right with the toy theatre when you were hidden from the audience behind the bed curtain and you could nudge your friend when it was his turn to speak, or read the words scribbled on a page, but here they were standing up in front of a real live audience and the whole thing suddenly seemed a lot more difficult.

It began well enough. James bounded on to the boiler top, struck a piratical attitude, and said:

'Ho, ho, my proud pirates. I spy a desert island.'

Jimmy Robb followed him and said:

'Aye, aye, cap'n. Methinks it is a desert island, to be sure, and methinks I'll bet there's treasure buried on it.'

'We'll land and find the treasure.'

'Aye, aye, cap'n. Methinks that's a good idea.'

'Lower the jolly boat.'

'Aye, aye, cap'n. Methinks – '

'Dinna keep sayin' "Methinks". It sounds silly.'

'I'm sorry, Jamie, but I canna right get the language unless I dae.'

'Well, try!'

The audience laughed and James hurried to launch out again in his character of the pirate captain.

'Bring your cutlasses. There may be natives.'

'Aye, aye, cap'n. Methinks –'

'There ye go again!'

'I wasna thinkin'.'

'I want four stout seamen tae row the jolly boat. See tae it.'

'Aye, aye, cap'n.'

'Methinks – Och! Ye've got me daein' it as well!'

By now the audience was in an uproar, cheering and whistling, and although the brave actors managed to quieten them, things began to go more and more wrong. For one thing, they suddenly found it was difficult to do a play with only two characters, and if either of them had to stop playing one part and begin playing someone completely different, they had to explain the change to the audience. Gradually things became very complicated and the audience lost the thread of the story. When that happened, those sitting on the hard floor began to offer suggestions and advice, and before long some of them were trying to join in the play.

The whole thing ended with James and Jimmy Robb fighting together to see which one of them could push the other into the boiler first.

Eventually Margaret and Jane Ann had to run from the house to see what the noise was about and to stop several different fights which had broken out amongst rival pirates in the audience. Gradually the audience sorted itself out and began to leave.

They had not seen a play, but they had all thoroughly enjoyed themselves.

That night James sat in his little box bed and

thought over the events in the washhouse that afternoon. He was not quite sure what had gone wrong, but he knew that he had a lot to learn about the difficult business of putting on a play.

6

Travel

James awoke and sat up in bed with a start. It was quite dark, and there was no sound except for the steady ticking of the wag-at-the-wall clock. In the pale moonlight filtering through the curtains he could see the clock's pendulum swinging steadily to and fro, and the black hands on the white face pointed at twenty minutes to one.

He wondered what had woken him.

There was no sound from outside. The Tenements were sleeping, and he could see in his mind's eye the whole of Kirriemuir lying along the banks of the Gairie Burn, its red stone houses pale in the silvery moonlight, silent and still. The shops and houses of Bank Street and the Kirk Wynd closed and shuttered with no light showing anywhere, and the Town House in the Square etched sharply black against the paler night sky. It gave him a funny excited feeling to think that he might be the only person awake in the whole town. He hugged the thought to him for a while, his knees drawn up under the blankets and his arms clasped round them.

Then from the room on the other side of the entrance door he heard the scrape of a chair on the stone flags of the floor.

James swung his legs out of bed, curling up his toes as his feet touched the cold floor. He pulled his stockings on hastily and tiptoed across to the door, avoiding the furniture of the crowded little room in the pale moonlight.

Sometimes his mother could not sleep and would wander round the house and Jane Ann had to follow her and persuade her to go back to bed. James knew that it was in the small hours of the morning that her distress over David was at its sharpest, making her roam restlessly from room to room, recalling memories of the happy days when David too had slept here.

Perhaps this time the ever-watchful Jane Ann had not heard Margaret leave her room upstairs. The girls would all be sound asleep in the other upstairs room, huddled under the blankets of their beds, unaware that their mother was again roaming the house.

James quietly lifted the latch of the door and peered

out. He glanced up the stairs and was surprised to see the door of his mother's room still tight shut. He looked across the little lobby and noticed a thin line of light round the opposite door.

Cautiously he lifted the latch and pushed the door open, blinking in the sudden glare of the oil lamp which burnt within.

His father sat at the table, his head resting on an open book. The table was covered with papers and books and Mr Barrie sat in his shirt sleeves, his jacket thrown over the back of his chair. He did not stir as James went in.

For a moment James stared at his father, and he felt a funny little shiver run up and down his spine. What was his father doing down here at this time of the night, still dressed, with books spread all over the table in front of him? And why was he sitting with his head resting on the table top, so still?

He gulped and hurried across to his father, suddenly afraid that something might have happened to him, and shook him by the shoulder.

'Father!' he whispered softly, so as not to disturb the sleeping household. 'Father! Are ye all right?'

Mr Barrie stirred and grunted.

'Eh?' he mumbled. 'Whassat? Who is it?'

He opened his eyes and blinked and then saw James standing over him.

'Why, hullo, Jamie,' he said and suddenly yawned cavernously. 'I must hae fallen asleep. What are ye daein' through here? What's the time?'

'It's near one o'clock, Father,' said James, answering the last question first. 'I woke up and heard a noise and I thought it might be Mother.'

'Eh, dearie me, I should hae been in my bed long

ago,' said Mr Barrie, and he pushed his knuckles into his eyes and rubbed. 'I fell asleep at my work.'

That surprised James, To him, his father's work was at the loom, and he wondered what he could have to do in the house.

Mr Barrie saw the look on James's face, and he suddenly lifted him up and set him down on the table top.

'Ye'd best sit up there and keep your feet out of the draught,' he said. He sat down again and stifled another yawn. 'Aye, my work, Jamie. Ye didna ken that I'm busy learnin' things, just like you at the school, eh?'

'No, Father.'

'Well, I am.'

Mr Barrie gestured a little wearily at the piles of books and papers in front of him. James picked up one of the books and looked at the title. *Practical Accountancy,* it said. He picked up another. *Keeping A Ledger.* He did not know what the titles meant, but the books looked very dry and uninteresting, full of strange rows of numbers and odd diagrams.

'What does it all mean, Father?' he asked.

'That's just what I'm tryin' tae find out myself, laddie,' said Mr Barrie with a chuckle. Then he became serious and for a moment or two sat fiddling with a bit of paper on the desk. James saw that he had some figures written on it in his own round handwriting. 'Dae ye feel wide enough awake for a wee talk?' asked Mr Barrie at last.

James felt himself thrill at the words. He so rarely saw his father, who spent his day working away at his loom to earn the money to keep the family, that the chance of talking with him was an unexpected treat, and even though he was beginning to feel sleepy again this was too good a chance to miss.

'*Aye,* Father!' he said eagerly.

'Good. Ye remember the Giant ye used tae be sae scared of? The mill we talked about?'

James nodded. He had not thought much about the Giant recently, because there had been so many other things to think of, and the Giant never seemed to arrive, anyway.

'Well, it's comin', said Mr Barrie.

'The Giant?'

'No, laddie. There's no Giant. The mill. The power mill that can make linen faster and better and finer than the handloom weavers can.'

'When, Father?'

'I dinna ken, but it's comin'. They're workin' them in Dundee, and already we handloom weavers in Kirrie-muir are feelin' the difference. The price we get for our linen is droppin'. Soon we'll not be able tae earn a livin' wage. The mills are takin' the work away from us. The handloom weavin's finished. There'll soon not be any men workin' away at their looms in their own houses. Folk will be workin' in big mills.'

'Will you hae tae work in a mill, Father?'

'It looks like it, Jamie. Mebbe not for some time yet, but when the time comes I want tae be ready for it. I've been hearin' stories about what's happened tae the weavers in Dundee. Dae ye ken, the mills there employ lassies tae run the machines?'

'Lassies in a mill?'

'That's right. It's easy for a lassie tae mind a machine, and that means that the men are out of work. Things hae got all tapsle-teerie in Dundee. In the old days the men worked the looms and the lassies knitted stockings. Now the lassies are mindin' the power looms and the men are knittin' stockings. That's nae job for a self-respectin' man tae dae.'

James thought of his mother and his sisters sitting in the evenings and the click of the needles as they knitted. He thought of the cottage doors of Kirriemuir where you could see on any fine day the woman of the house sitting in the sunshine on a three legged stool, working away at her needles. To him this was women's work, and the thought of his father sitting idly at home knitting stockings while Isabella and Sara and maybe even Jane Ann went out to a mill to watch the looms was one which he found hard to accept.

'Will you be knittin' stockings, Father?' he asked wonderingly.

'No, Jamie, I will not. I'll never dae that. And your sisters will never work in a mill if I can help it. That's why I'm studyin' every night here. When the mills come they'll be big, Jamie. And there'll be a lot of business passin' through them, and lots of money tae be handled. I'm tryin' tae learn how tae be a clerk, sae that I can get a job in the mill helpin' tae look after the business side of things.'

James looked at his father with wonder. It was hardly surprising that he had been looking tired for some time now! Working all day at the loom, trying, in spite of falling prices, to earn enough money for the family to live on, studying business methods from books at night. A man who until a few years ago had barely been able to read or to write, he was teaching himself a totally strange occupation alone in the evenings so that he would not be out of work when the mill came, but would be ready to step into a new kind of job. And he was not a young man. James knews he was over fifty.

He could not quite put these thoughts in clear order in his mind, but he looked at his father with a greater respect and a lot more affection even than he had done before.

'Can I help ye, Father?' he asked eagerly, anxious to show somehow that he appreciated the enormous labour his father was engaged in.

Mr Barrie chuckled and punched him playfully on the shoulder.

'I doubt ye couldna dae that, Jamie,' he said gently. 'I find it hard enough tae understand what it's all about myself, but I'm beginnin' tae see it. Aye, I'm beginnin' tae see it. When the time comes I think I'll be ready.'

He stopped suddenly and looked at his son thoughtfully.

'Mebbe I'm wrong,' he said. 'There is something ye can dae tae help, though not in the way ye might think.'

'Anything, Father!'

Mr Barrie rubbed his beard for a moment.

'Ye ken your brother Alexander has just got a job as classics master at Glasgow Academy?' he said.

'Aye.'

'That's a good job,' said Mr Barrie proudly. 'A very good job indeed. I had a letter from Alexander the other day, and he wants ye tae go and bide with him and study at Glasgow Academy.'

James felt a little knot of anxiety tugging at his stomach.

'Ye mean – ye mean like – like David did at Bothwell?'

A look of pain passed fleetingly across Mr Barrie's face.

'Aye,' he said. 'But Glasgow Academy's a different thing from Alexander's own school at Bothwell. It's one of the best schools in the country, Jamie, and ye'd get a fine lot of learnin' there.'

James wriggled uncomfortably on the table top. Glasgow was a huge place and he would be a little scared to be living there, even though Alexander would be there to look after him. Besides, who would watch over his mother and keep her happy and cheerful if he was not here to do it?

'But Mother –' he said.

'Aye,' said Mr Barrie. 'I doubt your mother wouldna be happy tae see ye go. Especially after what happened ... Still, I'm sure she would agree tae it if she thought ye were anxious tae go yourself.'

Mr Barrie looked at James very pointedly.

'Ye see, Jamie, I've told ye about the handloom weavin' and how things arena very good for us now. It would make things easier for me if ye went tae Alexander. It's not that I want ye tae go away from us. Dinna think that, for it's not true. But for just now, till times get easier, we could manage much better here if there was one less mouth tae feed. It's very kind of Alexander tae offer tae take ye. He kens things arena just at their best for us, and it's his way of helpin' out.'

James felt himself being torn in two different directions at the same time. On the one hand was the thought that it would help his father if he went away, and also that he would get a good education at Glasgow. On the other was the frightening thought of leaving Kirriemuir and the life he knew so well, and of leaving his mother with no one to watch over her and keep her from thinking sad thoughts. True, Jane Ann would look after her, but Jane Ann was not able to prevent her from being sad the way he could. There was also the thought that the happy evenings when he sat and

listened to her stories of the bygone days of the Auld
Licht Church worthies would be gone, perhaps for ever.
It was not an easy decision for an eight year old boy
to take.

His father was watching him, and there was a lot of
sympathy in the steady eyes.

'I've aye wished that I had had an education,' he
said. 'Learnin's a great thing, Jamie. Tae be able tae
read difficult books and understand what the writer
mannie means, and tae be able tae write a good round
hand and put your own thoughts down on paper, man,
I think that must be one of the greatest things in the
world.'

A coal dropped in the dying embers of the fire and
sudden shadows sprang up and danced on the wall
opposite the grate.

'Alexander's had that education,' said Mr Barrie. 'He
has a degree with what they call First Class Honours in
Classics, and I'm told that's not an easy thing tae get.
Your brother David would hae had the same kind of
education. I would like tae see my other son get the
same chance.'

Silence fell between them. James sat staring into the
red glow of the fire, his mind in a whirl. He was still
being pulled in two directions, but he knew now the
direction he was going to go in. It was not the way he
wanted to go, but it was the right one.

He licked his lips and swallowed.

'All right, Father,' he whispered. 'I'd – I'd like fine
tae go tae Glasgow.'

Mr Barrie smiled at him.

'That's my laddie,' he said approvingly. 'Alexander
will look after ye, and your sister Mary's keepin' house
for him, sae really it'll be like bein' with part of the

family anyway. But, Jamie, just between you and me, make your mother think ye're really keen tae go. All right?'

James nodded.

'I ken how close the pair of ye are, and that's a good thing. Ye've done a lot for her since David died, Jamie, and I'm grateful tae ye for that. I've never spoken tae ye of it before, and mebbe I should hae done, but I want ye tae ken how grateful I am. If it hadna been for you she might not hae got over it. But because ye're sae close, it might be difficult for me tae persuade her tae let ye go, d'ye see? If she thinks you're keen, she'll not stand in your way.'

'All right, Father,' said James.

Mr Barrie stood up and stretched stiffly. Then he lifted James gently down from the table.

'Now it's bed for you and me both, my lad,' he said. 'Ye can hardly keep your eyes open, and tae tell ye the truth, I'm not much better myself.'

And indeed, having made his decision, James suddenly felt very tired. It was as though there were heavy weights pulling on his eyelids, trying to force them shut, and he could not stifle a yawn. He was hardly aware of his father taking him through to the next room and tucking him into his bed, though that was something which he had never done before.

He was asleep almost before his head touched the pillow.

*

James was enrolled at Glasgow Academy on 19th August 1868.

Alexander brought him from Kirriemuir. They boarded the same train which David had boarded nearly two years before, and James had a funny feeling as he leant out of the carriage window and waved to his mother and father and Isabella and Sara and Jane Ann and little Margaret as they grew smaller on the receding platform, that this was an exact repeat of the scene on that day, only this time it was he who was in the carriage instead of David and there was no small boy standing on the platform with the rest of the family who might see the suspicious glint of tears in his eyes.

But this time it was different, because this time Alexander was in the carriage as well, sitting solidly on the seat opposite him, dressed in a neat tweed suit and puffing at a pipe and smiling at him encouragingly. Alexander knew the wrench it was to leave his home and his family.

They swayed and clattered along the single line to Forfar. There they changed trains and waited on the platform for the Aberdeen–Glasgow express. Soon they were rattling and panting westwards and James, who had never been so far from Kirriemuir before soon forgot the wave of homesickness and sat entranced at the changing scenery outside the carriage window. They stopped at Perth and Stirling and some time later they reached the outskirts of Glasgow. James was fascinated and rather frightened by the big grimy factories with their tall chimneys belching smoke on either side of the line, and by the rows of mean little tenement houses which peeped shyly between them. The houses were no bigger than the Kirriemuir house he had just left, but they seemed smaller because they were so cramped together and piled on top of one another that he wondered how people could breathe in them.

At the Buchanan Street station Alexander hailed a cab and soon they were clip-clopping along the cobbles of the Cowcaddens and into the New City Road. The streets were thronged with carriages and the pavements crowded with people. Everything seemed very dirty and James felt he could almost taste the soot in the air he breathed.

Just beyond St George's Cross the cab turned into Burnbank Terrace and left the bustle of the city behind them. It was a street of tall terraced houses with big windows. As the cab drew to a halt outside one of these houses James saw his sister Mary waiting on the doorstep to greet him.

It should have been like coming to a second home, but the city was too strange and new and big and noisy for James to feel it anything like the quiet Kirriemuir which he had left only that morning.

Somehow he never did learn to like Glasgow, and the longer he spent there the more he longed for Kirriemuir and the quiet places he knew so well.

He did reasonably well at school, but he made few friends there, perhaps because the other pupils were a little shy of the boy whose brother was the imposing classics master, and James always looked forward to the holidays when he could return home.

It was not that Alexander and Mary neglected him in any way. No one could have been kinder than they were, and he and Alexander would go for long walks at the weekends, taking the road westwards over the Kelvin Bridge and past the big Academy building standing on the north bank of the river into the quiet countryside beyond Hillhead and Jordanhill. On these occasions Alexander did not act like a schoolmaster at all, and James enjoyed the company of his bluff, hearty brother. But even this was not the same as fishing in the Prosen or rambling out on the Brechin Road with his friends to Tannadice seven miles away.

He did his school work thoroughly though not out-standingly, but the highlights of the three years he spent at Glasgow Academy were his trips home in the holidays and one of these trips was to stand out especi-ally in his memory.

7

Flitting

The day which David Barrie had long been preparing for arrived in the early summer of 1870.

The Giant came to Forfar. The enormous Laird's Mill opened that year and Mr Barrie applied for, and got, a position as clerk in the office there. This meant that the family would have to leave the Tenements and go to live in the county town.

James was at home, on holiday from the Glasgow

Academy when the 'flitting' took place. His presence in
the house in the Tenements was a great relief to Jane
Ann, because their mother was not well and yet would
insist on trying to help with the packing of all the
precious family belongings. It was as much as Jane
Ann could do to make her stay in her bed which had
been moved to Bell Lunan's house next door. She was
to stay there until the removal was complete and the
new home in Forfar ready to receive her.

The day of the flitting was fine and bright, and
there was general relief all round, for it would not
have been much fun packing all the furniture into the
carrier's cart and accompanying it the six miles to Forfar if it had been raining.

The whole family was awake even earlier than usual
that morning. Jane Ann roused them all at about five
o'clock when the sun had barely risen above the roof-
tops, and after a hasty breakfast James helped Jane
Ann and Isabella and Sara and little Margaret to move
the furniture out of the house and into the yard. Jane
Ann ran from room to room, advising, helping, dart-
ing off to make sure that everything was going well,
occasionally running across to Bell Lunan's house to
see that their mother was still in her bed, for Margaret
had taken it into her head to get up and help, and
Bell, crippled as she was and unable to move without
the aid of her stick, would not have been able to prevent her.

It seemed strange to see all the furniture standing
nakedly in the yard, exposed to the light of day and
the gaze of anyone who cared to look in.

When everything was out, James went back into
the little house and wandered on his own from room
to room. It seemed so much bigger now that it was

empty of furniture, and the rooms echoed to the sound of his footsteps. He saw the brighter patch on a wall where a picture had hung, the blackness of the grate in the parlour with none of the ornaments on the mantel to break up the line. Upstairs was the same story. The house was stripped, and suddenly it seemed to be nothing more than a collection of small rooms with low ceilings, not a home where the family had lived all his life, where they had shared joys and sorrows and the secrets which all families have. The things that made a house a home were outside now, the pots and pans, the little treasured ornaments, the pictures, the books, and of course the hair-bottomed chairs, but most particularly the people.

Nevertheless he felt a sharp pang of regret that this, the only home he had ever known, was not his any longer, and that he was to go to a new house, one he had never seen before, in a new town where he would have to pick up the threads of his life again.

The clatter of hooves of the carrier's horse broke in on his thoughts and he hurried out of his mother's old bedroom, down the steep narrow stairs for the last time, and out blinking into the sunlight of the yard.

'Good morning, Geordie,' he called, as the cart pulled to a halt beside the pile of furniture.

''Mornin', young Jamie,' said Geordie.

He was more bent than he had been ten years before when he had brought the hair-bottomed chairs to the house for the first time, but James was not to know that. He jumped stiffly down from the cart and surveyed the pile of furniture with his hands on his hips.

'Is that it?' he asked.

'That's everything, Geordie,' said Jane Ann.

Geordie grunted.

'I'm glad tae hear it,' he said. 'There's an awful amount of stuff there. D'ye think ye're goin' tae get that all in one load?'

Jane Ann blinked. It had to go in one load. If they had to send Geordie back from Forfar to Kirriemuir for another load it would cost them a lot more money, and although David Barrie had a new secure job with a steady wage, and a much larger one than any he had earned as a handloom weaver, the habit of thrift and economy which Jane Ann and her mother had toiled under for so long was not easy to forget.

'I thought ye were so clever at packin' things on tae the cart, Geordie, that there'd be nae difficulty in gettin' everything on,' she said in a tone of great surprise.

Geordie grunted and accepted the challenge.

'Aye, well, mebbe,' he said. 'We'll see, we'll see.'

The children gathered round to help, and Geordie directed them, selecting different articles to fill up space on the cart so that every square inch would be used.

'Pass me that chair, Isabella,' he would say. 'No, not *that* chair, ye gomeril. How are ye goin' tae fit that muckle great thing intae a wee space the like of this? *That* one. That's better.'

'Mind the polish on that table!' Jane Ann would cry suddenly.

'Aye, if ye're worried about the polish ye shouldna hae sae much stuff tae go on the cart,' Geordie would retort.

The packing-up went on swiftly, nevertheless, and when it was nearly done James slipped through to Bell Lunan's house to see his mother.

Looking pale and worried she was sitting up in bed in Bell's front room where she commanded a view of the Brechin Road through the front window, the window at which Bell usually sat to watch life passing by outside.

'Is everything all right, Jamie?' she asked, her fingers plucking nervously at the coverlet, and James knew that if she were given half a chance she would leap out of bed and advance into the yard in her nightdress to supervise the loading of the cart. He hastened to set her mind at rest.

'Everything's fine, Mother,' he said. 'Jane Ann and Geordie are managing everything.'

'I never did trust that Geordie,' said Margaret. 'I'm near certain it was him that scratched the chair the day your father carried them intae the house. Ye're sure he's not scratchin' it now? There's nothing broken, is there? I'm sure I heard a crash just now.'

'Nothing's broken at all and they're being very careful. We'll all be in tae say goodbye tae ye in a wee while, and then ye'll see the cart goin' down the road, and can see for yourself that everything's just fine.'

Margaret lay back, almost reassured, but suddenly she put a hand on James's arm.

'The chairs,' she said. 'Ye'll take good care of my six chairs? Such a time I had savin' sixpences and bawbees from the housekeepin' money tae pay for them!'

'We're takin' extra special care of the chairs.'

'Now that your father's got this braw new job I expect we'll be able tae buy much grander chairs, but I've got a liking for the old ones. They were the first things we bought that were really our very own . . .'

'Mother, the only way the chairs would get hurt would be if someone took an axe tae them.'

'The axe!' said Margaret suddenly. 'Jamie, dinna forget the axe! It's in the washhouse just tae the right of the door. We'll need that for choppin' firewood at the new house –'

'The axe is in the cart already. I put it there myself.'

When James had eventually calmed her down he went back to the yard to find the last of the household articles being carefully placed on top of the cart and Geordie was busy with ropes, tying everything securely down.

Each of them had a last look round the house, the washhouse and the yard to make sure that nothing had been left, and then they all went in to Bell Lunan's house to say goodbye to their mother while Geordie turned the cart.

The arrival of the family started Margaret off on a string of instructions, mainly to Jane Ann, about what to do when they reached Forfar, and even as they left the house her voice followed them with last minute orders to be good and to help Jane Ann and not to upset any of the Forfar folk. There was supposed to have been great rivalry between the two towns ever since the handloom weaving started so she wanted to be sure that none of them got into any trouble. She also told them to make sure they put on dry shoes and stockings if they came in when it was wet.

Gleefully they climbed aboard the cart, scrambling over the piled up furniture to find nesting places at the top, while Jane Ann told them not to scratch anything with their big feet, and Geordie growled that they would upset the load if they weren't careful. James found himself a little nook on top of a rug with his head against the side of a dresser and his feet dangling over the edge of the cart.

The horse strained and pulled and the cart began to rumble out of the yard, through Lilybank on to the

Brechin Road, and there turned left to go through the town.

Through Bell Lunan's window they caught sight of their mother waving anxiously to them. They waved back and shouted that everything was fine, but James was sure from the look on her face that she did not believe that was possible.

The flitting had begun.

Friends and neighbours called good luck to them as they passed along Bank Street and into the Square, passing the Town House on their right and down the road to the bridge over the Gairie. There Geordie stopped.

'I'm not carryin' the lot of ye up the brae,' he said. 'The horse has enough tae manage without your weight as well. Ye'll need tae get down and lend a hand tae push at the back.'

They scrambled down, Jane Ann as well, and Geordie got off to lead the horse up the steep brae of the Commonty to Southmuir. The cart creaked and groaned its way up the slope, the children pushing from behind to help the horse with his load, and at the top they clambered back to their places again.

James looked back at the little town, spread out in steps along the steep bank of the Gairie on the north side, and wondered with a slight pang if he would ever see Kirriemuir again, but it did not last, for the flitting ahead of them was too exciting for him to feel sad for long.

Where the Glamis road branched off from the Forfar road they turned left, and soon they were lurching steadily along between green hedges bright with gowans, and the fields beyond were a lush green with growing crops. A fresh breeze blew in from the east and high white clouds chased across a blue sky, dappling the land in sun and shadow.

In an hour the roofs and spires of Forfar were drawing close, and James felt like an explorer in one of his stories who was approaching a strange new land. He looked about him eagerly. The cart passed through the little village of Zoar and within a few minutes the outskirts of Forfar were passing on either side.

Eventually the cart turned off into a lane which Geordie told them was called the Limepots, and in a little while they drew to a halt beside a high stone wall with a door in it which stood open and showed steps leading up to the kailyard or garden which stood higher than the road. Beyond the garden rose the creeper clad house, and to James's eyes it seemed enormous after the Tenements in Kirriemuir.

'Is this it?' he asked.

Jane Ann nodded.

'Aye, this is it, Jamie. Our new home. Come on. Let's help Geordie get the furniture in. Father'll be here soon. He's at the new mill this morning, but they're giving him time off tae help with the flitting.'

But before any work could be done the children had to explore the new house, and for some time the empty rooms echoed with their shouts and gasps of delight.

There were four rooms, the same as there had been at the Tenements, but they were bigger and there was a proper entrance hall and a wide and more spacious flight of stairs to the second floor, and of course there was the kailyard, full of vegetables and bushes and trees, and James knew immediately that this kailyard would be a wonderful place to explore, a place in which to be a pirate stepping through unconquered

jungle or maybe a Jacobite jinking through the heather
to escape the redcoats.

Soon the furniture was carried in while Jane Ann,
flushed and breathless and a little anxious, directed
where each article should be put. James struggled
under the bulk of a feather mattress, and then
helped Geordie lift in the dresser. Jane Ann herself
brought in the six hair-bottomed chairs, and Isabella
and Sara proudly bore in tables and bedding. Even little
Margaret staggered up the steps from the road and
through the kailyard with her arms full of pots and
pans for the new kitchen just to the right of the entrance
door.

Some time later they stood at the garden steps and
watched Geordie, fortified with a 'jeely piece' and a
cup of tea, drive the empty cart away down the lane
and back to Kirriemuir, and with this last link with
their old town broken they turned and prepared to
begin the new life in Forfar.

*

Margaret Ogilvy was fit enough to make the journey
to the new house three weeks later, and shortly after
that James regretfully returned to Glasgow for the new
term.

But he was not to complete the session there. That
year Alexander resigned as classics master at the Glasgow Academy. The reason was that the new Education
Act was shortly coming into force, and Alexander had
been promised a position of Inspector of Schools, an
important job in which he would have to travel around
the area to which he was appointed to make sure that
the schools were all properly run according to the new
Government ruling. He did not know where he would
become an inspector, but in the meantime he felt it

would be wise to learn something about the new job, and so he took a post as inspector to the Free Church Schools Board to give himself an idea of what he would be required to do.

This meant him leaving Glasgow, so James could no longer stay with him. He returned to Forfar and was enrolled as a pupil at Forfar Academy.

He felt more at home in Forfar than he had ever done in Glasgow. For one thing he was back with his family, and for another he was near the part of the country he knew best. The people he met spoke in the same way a way as he did and did not make fun of his accent, and he could understand what everyone said which was sometimes not easy with the polite sing-song of Glasgow's Kelvinside or the nasal whine of the poorer areas.

Overcoming the shyness which had grown in him in the strangeness of Glasgow, he made many friends and so had a new audience for his stories. On a fine summer afternoon he would stroll home from school with a friend, quite unaware of his surroundings, while he told the story of Sir Walter Scott's great novel *Ivanhoe* which he had just read. So vivid was his description of the characters and the action that his friend would declare James's version to be better than the original, but because of James's telling of the story he would develop a love of Scott which would last him all his life. If the story was unfinished when they reached the house in the Limepots the two boys would climb the steps to the kailyard and sit in the warm sunshine on the grass in front of the house, James talking and making gestures as he explained a part of the story, their heads close together. Margaret, watching them from the parlour window, would smile and shake her head.

'Jamie's fillin' another laddie's head with his tales,' she would say to Jane Ann.

There was an air of security about the household now. No longer was there the grey fear of unemployment or falling income hanging over them. No longer did Mr Barrie have to work at his handloom from dawn till dusk as long as the light lasted, weaving linen for customers who paid him less and less for his labour. He had a regular job with regular hours, the drawn tired look disappeared from his face and the heavy dark lines under his eyes faded.

Now he could spend more time with his family than he had ever been able to do before. The family seemed closer knit than ever, and they formed a comfortable, happy little circle.

But before two years had passed the Giant had taken another step northwards, and what Mr Barrie had long expected to happen did happen. A power mill opened in Kirriemuir. On a stretch of flat ground on the north bank of the little Gairie Burn rose the big buildings and the tall chimney which would belch smoke over the red stone houses.

Mr Barrie had done well at his new, self-taught job, and when the Gairie Mill at Kirriemuir opened in the summer of 1872 he was appointed confidential clerk to the directors, a job which brought in more money even than he had earned in Forfar.

So one again the family flitted, this time in the other direction, but they did not return to the Tenements. A new house had been built at Southmuir, on the south bank of the burn, a fine red stone house overlooking the town to the north. It was called Strathview, and Mr Barrie rented the top flat of this house for his family.

No more the Tenements yard and the washhouse for

a playground, no more the little low ceilinged rooms and the tiny windows. This was a really grand house with big, high rooms and big windows letting in lots of light, with a fine view on all sides, and a big garden.

A big house like this would need new furniture and new carpets and new curtains, but now it was not a matter of counting the pennies to see which of these was most important and which they could afford. Mr Barrie could still not spend money like water, of course, but compared with what they had had in the old Kirriemuir days, they were very comfortably off. The days of making do, of turning old clothes into new, were gone for ever. There was no need to haggle with the flesher over the price of beef, though from long habit Margaret Ogilvy continued to do so. Gradually new pieces of furniture were added to the new house, though the hair-bottomed chairs still occupied a favoured position in the parlour.

James was delighted to be back in his home town once more, though now the Giant had come in earnest. At half past five every morning the factory whistle roused him from sleep and the clatter of the lassies' feet as they made their way to work through the faint half-light or the deep dark cold of winter echoed along the streets.

And it was the lassies who were earning the money now. The old handloom weavers had to sit back knitting stockings as Mr Barrie said they would. James would sometimes see them sitting outside their doors on a fine day, their needles flashing in the sun, and a faraway sad look in their eyes as they thought of the independence and the craft which had died with the coming of the power mill. They had fought for many years to keep their independence, but this Giant set up suddenly in their midst was something they could not fight. And James thought how wise his father had been to teach himself to become a clerk so that he too was not sitting knitting stockings while his daughters ran to their looms at the mill in the early morning.

There were changes in Kirriemuir besides this most obvious one. The power mill and the business it brought to the town brought a new life to the place as well. Time no longer passed slowly, as it had done. People no longer had time to stop and gossip at their doors for hours on end. An air of purpose had arrived. People's steps were brisker, the old ways were dying.

James saw this, and thought of the change he had seen in the short twelve years of his life. And he thought too of the changes there had been since his mother's girlhood, since the days of the Auld Licht Church and the worthies who had made up its congregation. And he wondered in himself whether these changes were altogether a good thing and whether there was not something in the old ways which was worth preserving.

8

Dumfries

It was in the garret at Strathview at the age of twelve
that James Barrie decided that a life of literature was to
be his. He told his mother of his decision, and she nodded encouragingly but a little absently, for she was busy
baking.

'I daresay ye'll dae it, Jamie,' she said. 'But it's not an
easy life, I'm told. Ye'll need tae stick in tae your
lessons.'

This was difficult, because at the moment James had no lessons to 'stick in' to.

Margaret was humouring him. Writing was all very well, but it was terribly insecure, and she was sure that no one could ever earn a respectable living at it. Privately she hoped that her son might become a minister, like her brother was. She was very proud of the Rev. David Ogilvy the little boy she had brought up from the age of five and who now had a parish in Motherwell. James had actually visited his uncle there while he had been in Glasgow and he remembered the visit very clearly because it was the first house he had been to where a servant was kept. When he arrived at his uncle's house the first thing he did was to make his way to the kitchen and peep round the door to see if the servant really existed and find out what sort of strange animal a servant was.

Margaret of course had never had a servant, but the knowledge that her brother was able to keep one and her admiration for David Ogilvy made her hope that James might become a minister too.

But she was too wise to suggest it at the present time when his enthusiastic young mind was totally taken up with thoughts of becoming a famous writer of serial stories about Sweeney Todd and Dick Turpin and Spring-heeled Jack, the heroes of the magazines he thrilled to.

In the year the Barries moved back to Kirriemuir, Alexander was appointed Inspector of Schools in the Dumfries area and once again he offered to take James under his wing, send him to Dumfries Academy and have him live in the house which he had just taken in the town.

The offer was accepted, for there was no suitable school in Kirriemuir now for James, and Forfar Academy was too far away for him to travel there every day.

So James spent only a year at Strathview after the family's return from Forfar before setting off again, this time to the far south-west of Scotland.

*

Dumfries, unlike Glasgow, seemed a second home to James right from the day he arrived. To begin with he was not quite sure why this was, but it only took him a short time to find out. It was mainly because the houses in the town were built of the same kind of red stone as the houses in Kirriemuir, so that although the town was much bigger it seemed in some ways familiar.

The countryside round about was much the same too, though perhaps a little softer than the Forfar fields and hills, and the River Nith which ran through Dumfries to the Solway Firth a few miles away was a great deal bigger than the Gairie Burn. But there was fishing in the Nith and the Cairn, and there were walks to Caerlaverock Castle and Sweetheart Abbey.

There were literary associations with the town, too, which suited James. The famous philosopher, Thomas Carlyle had been born in Ecclefechan a little to the east, and he was sometimes to be seen stalking through the streets of Dumfries in his wide hat and cloak with a stick in his hand, a grim-looking figure who filled James with a sense of fear and awe. He never spoke to James, for Carlyle rarely spoke to anyone.

And of course Robert Burns had lived in Dumfries when he worked as an exciseman and had died there in 1796. Two of the first places James visited were the poet's grave in a corner of St Michael's Churchyard, and the house where he had died.

D

There was history here, too, in plenty. The Monastery of the Greyfriars used to stand where Castle Street now stands, and although there was nothing left of it, James found the spot where Robert the Bruce had slain the Red Comyn in the Church of the Greyfriars and so made his claim to the Scottish throne which sparked off the Wars of Independence against Edward I of England.

Alexander had taken a house in Victoria Terrace near the railway station. It was a red stone house with square windows standing right on the road edge with a garden on the opposite side, and from his bedroom window James could see the trains steaming in and out of the station, heading for Glasgow in the north or Carlisle and London to the south. He would sit and watch the trains pulling out of the station, heading for Carlisle, see them steam under the bridge and clank past the sheds, gathering speed, their windows full of men in top hats and ladies in their best bonnets, heading into the mysterious land south of the border. He thought of the distances they had to travel to reach London and wondered if he would ever see London himself.

As the time passed he became more and more determined that one day he would go to London, which seemed to him to be the centre of literature and of everything which he felt was worthwhile. He had never been there, but like Dick Whittington he almost believed that the pavements were made of gold and that great opportunities awaited the brave explorer who ventured to the city.

He would stand on the railway bridge and look down at the shining rails curving away towards Carlisle and think to himself:

'That line doesna stop till it gets tae London.'

Dumfries Academy was accounted one of the twelve

best schools in Scotland, and in a country whose educational standards were far ahead of those in England at that time, this was saying a great deal. It was a fairly small square building which housed a little over two hundred pupils near the river, and here James began his studies again in the autumn of 1873.

Despite his growing shyness he made a lot of friends, mainly because of his impish sense of humour and also because he was always ready to join in any of the ploys which his companions got up to. In fact, after a while he began to lead many of these ploys himself.

His shyness grew from the fact that as he became older he found he was not growing so fast as his friends. He had never been a big boy, but as time passed he saw all those of his own age shooting past him in height and size while he stayed very much the same.

Alexander comforted him.

'Never you heed, Jamie,' he said. 'Remember, size isna everything. It's what's inside a man that counts. Besides, you'll see. You're a slow grower. Some day soon ye'll suddenly shoot up like a weed in a garden and ye'll be as tall as everyone else. The others have just shot up before ye, that's all.'

But James never did shoot up. He used to look at his friends and realise that he was having to raise his eyes higher and higher to be able to look them in the face. He sometimes wondered if this smallness was a punishment for wishing in earlier days that he need never grow up, because in fact although he was growing older, he was not growing in size.

This question of his smallness worried him and made him shy and reserved on occasions, but in spite of that he could be a great friend when he forgot about his

stature and joined in games and expeditions with the
others.

In one sphere he still had no equal, and that was in
the telling of stories. He used to read many of the comic
papers, not only the halfpenny magazine which had been
his only reading matter in Kirriemuir. More and more
of the 'penny dreadfuls' found their way into his
pockets, and he devoured the stories enthusiastically and
retold them to his friends, adding little touches of his
own when he felt it was necessary.

Near the Academy stood the house of two school
friends of his, Hal and Stuart Gordon. Their father,
Henry Gordon, was Sheriff Clerk and the family lived
in a big house called Moat Brae which had enormous
gardens reaching down to the River Nith. There were
many trees in these gardens and the boys used to play
in the trees after school, pretending they were on a
desert island and finding coconuts in the tree tops to eat.
The green apples they consumed caused many an upset
stomach the following day!

In the High Street, where the Midsteeple stood firmly
planted in the middle of the road, was a bookshop. This
was a real bookshop, not like Mr Mills's little shop in
Bank Street in Kirriemuir. It had a library attached to
it, and Mr Anderson, the owner, allowed James the run
of the shop and the book-filled attics above. Here he
spent many hours and discovered the joys not only of
melodramatic pirate and Red Indian stories, but of more
serious literature as well.

Mr Anderson had a son at the Academy and James
and Wellwood Anderson became firm friends. This
friendship was to mean a great deal to James during his
time at school.

*

'Good shot!'

The crisp crack of bat on ball was followed by a ripple of applause round the ground. James lay on his stomach, a notebook in front of him, chewing the end of a pencil as he watched the ball streak for the boundary.

It was a hot, sunny day and the Dumfries Academy cricket team was playing a match against another local school. James had been lying in his shirt sleeves, his jacket beside him, since the match began. Their opponents had batted first and made 187, which was a big score to beat, especially as the opposition had a huge boy who bowled at a tremendous pace and terrified the batsmen facing him. Already the Academy had lost four wickets for 42, and looked to be in real trouble. James had seen Wellwood dismissed for four, but now two other boys were making a stand taking the score carefully but steadily upwards into the nineties. It was beginning to look as though the result might at least be a draw. James hardly dared to hope that they could win.

He scribbled an illegible note in his book, and then returned to watching the game, his eyes screwed up against the strong sunlight. Really, that fast bowler was a demon . . .

A shadow fell across his notebook and he looked up to see Wellwood drop to the ground beside him.

'Ye didna dae sae well,' James observed.

Wellwood grunted.

'It was a beast of a ball,' he said. 'Swung away late and just caught the edge of my bat.'

'Well done, Dougie!' yelled James suddenly.

One of the batsmen lifted a ball clean back over the fast bowler's head to the boundary. The umpire raised both hands high.

'A six!' cried James.

He scribbled again in his notebook, while Wellwood watched him with interest.

'What are ye daein'?' he asked.

James blushed slightly.

'Och, I'm just tryin' something,' he said.

'Ye're not scorin', are ye?'

'No, no. I'm just – well – that is – Och, I'm goin' tae try writin' a report of the match for *The Dumfries Standard.*'

'Ye are?' said Wellwood with a note of admiration in his voice.

'I dinna ken if they'll take it or not, but I feel someone should write a report for the local paper, so I'm goin' tae hae a wee shottie.'

'A wee shottie!' scoffed Wellwood. 'Man, Jamie, are ye never goin' tae lose that Kirriemuir accent of yours?'

'Why should I? It's better than yours!'

'It is not, then!'

' 'Course it is!'

'All right, all right, it is. It's far too hot tae fight.'

'Aye, ye're right.'

Another scatter of applause broke out round the ground and the two boys joined in as the batsmen scampered a quick single and the hundred went up.

'They're daein' well, Dougie and Stuart,' said Wellwood. 'Dae ye think mebbe we might win?'

'We're gettin' awful short of time,' said James. 'We need eighty-eight runs in just under an hour. We could.'

They were silent for a while as they watched the demon fast bowler start his long run up to the wicket. The batsman stood patting his bat in the crease. The bowler reached the stumps and uncoiled himself like a spring, arms whirling. The batsman leapt out of his crease and swung his bat wildly. Had he connected the ball would have landed in the Nith, but he missed completely. The wicket keeper caught the ball and whipped off the bails. The fielders leapt in the air and there was a loud roar:

'Howzzat?'

The umpire's finger went up and the batsman began his slow, disappointed walk back to the edge of the ground.

'Bad luck, Stuart!' shouted Wellwood.

James scribbled again in his notebook and then turned to watch the next batsman walk to the crease.

The wicket had fallen at the end of the over. The opposition captain brought on a slow bowler at the other end, and the new batsman had only to stand and watch the slaughter during the next six balls. Dougie, as though to punish the opposing team for taking his partner's wicket hit twenty runs off the over, and the Dumfries Academy's chance of winning the match seemed a lot brighter. Dougie's score had now reached 61.

'Ye'll need tae give Dougie a good report in your article,' said Wellwood.

'I will,' said James.

'Dinna be too hard on me, will ye, Jamie?' said Wellwood with a grin.

'If ye're very respectful I'll try tae be nice tae ye,' said James solemnly.

Wellwood glanced at him, not quite sure if he was being serious or not. That was the trouble with James sometimes. You could never be sure when he was being funny, his face always remained absolutely straight.

The time crept on and the score mounted slowly but steadily. Two more wickets fell, but Dougie advanced into the eighties.

'I'm goin' tae start a magazine,' said Wellwood suddenly.

'Eh?' said James, startled out of his concentration on the cricket.

'Aye. Just a wee magazine in the school.'

'Ye mean ye'll get it printed?'

'No. That'd cost an awful lot of money. It'll just be done in handwriting and folk'll pay a halfpenny tae get a read at it.'

James felt a little disappointed. A magazine hardly seemed to be a magazine if it was not printed properly.

'What are ye goin' tae call it?' he asked.

'I havena right decided yet,' said Wellwood.

'Ye'll need a good title,' said James shrewdly. 'Something that'll make folk want tae read it.'

'Aye. I'll need tae think about that. Will ye write something for it, Jamie?'

'Gosh, I'd like tae, Wellwood.'

'Good. Mebbe one of your stories about pirates and things.'

'No. I dinna think sae. If it's a school magazine it'll need tae hae something tae dae with the school. I'll need tae think about it.'

Dougie's score was 96 and the Academy were 169 for 7, still needing 19 runs to win. The opposing captain had been forced to rest his demon fast bowler, but now he decided to bring him back and see if he could break this partnership which was beginning to grow a little too strong. He was now desperate to get the last three wickets, for there were only ten minutes left for play.

The fast bowler hurled himself in and let go of the ball. Dougie took a tremendous swipe at it and there was a roar from the fielders as his middle stump careered out of the ground, cartwheeling over the wicket keeper's head to land quivering with its pointed end stuck in the ground fifteen yards away.

'Och, Dougie, ye clown!' shouted James, almost as distressed as the batsman himself at being so near a century and missing it by four runs.

Dougie walked off the field, banging his bat on the ground in disgust at himself and the ninth batsman made his way out to the crease. James scribbled in his notebook and then became aware of Wellwood staring at him.

'What's the matter?' he asked.

'That's it,' said Wellwood. 'That's it! *The Clown.* That's what I'll call the magazine!'

'Oh, that,' said James, his mind fixed on what he was going to say in his report about Dougie's great innings which had ended so disappointingly.

'It's a great title,' said Wellwood. 'It sounds comic, and folk like the idea of readin' comic things. *The Clown.* That's the title, Jamie, my lad!'

But James was hardly listening. The drama of the cricket match was taking up all his attention. There could not be more than three overs to go after this one in which Dougie's wicket had fallen. Nineteen runs to make. The next ball flew off the edge of the bat between the slips and went for four. The Academy boys groaned aloud at the close shave, but four runs were valuable. Fifteen to win.

Stolidly the batsman played out the rest of the over without scoring.

The first ball of the next over nearly brought a wicket. The batsman skied the ball, a fielder got underneath it and dropped it to the sound of cheers from the Academy boys and the groans of his own supporters. Meanwhile the batsmen scampered through for a single.

The tension mounted. When the last over started the Academy needed seven runs to win, and there was a hush round the ground. James felt himself trembling slightly with excitement. Could they do it? Even if they couldn't, it was a most exciting finish and should make a wonderful report for the local paper. That would give him more chance of having the report accepted for printing.

The batsman dropped the first ball down in front of him and they raced through for a single. The second ball was treated the same way, but a fielder picked up the ball and shied it at the wicket as the batsmen crossed. He missed, and the ball went for two overthrows.

Three runs to win and four balls to go . . .

The next ball was a beauty and the batsman could do nothing except keep it off his wicket. The ball after that was so far outside the off stump that he could not reach it and the umpire signalled a wide. They ran a single off the second last ball and the scores were level. Then, amidst a dead silence the fielders flexed their muscles to stop any run off the last ball. Just one needed to win. The bowler ran up to the wicket and let fly. The ball was down the leg side, the batsman followed it round and connected cleanly. Amidst scenes of wild rejoicing they crossed for the single while one of the fielders tore after the ball in a vain attempt to prevent a run.

'Whew!' said Wellwood as the pitch was suddenly invaded by a horde of delighted Academy boys. 'We won! But it was close!'

'It certainly was,' said James as he felt himself relax after the tension. He scribbled in his notebook and then got to his feet.

'Now I'll need tae write out my report and hand it in to *The Dumfries Standard* office,' he said.

'I hope they take it, Jamie,' said Wellwood. 'And remember *The Clown.*'

'The what?'

'*The Clown.* The magazine. I want ye tae write something for it.'

'Oh, aye. That. All right, Wellwood, I'll see what I
can dae.'

*

Some days later James stood trembling at the door of
The Dumfries Standard office, waiting for the new edition to come off the press. He had written his report and
when he handed it in to the office it had seemed good to
him, but since then he had become more and more unhappy about it until he was almost sure that the editor
would never print it.

When the first copies arrived on the counter he seized
one and almost got away without paying for it until the
clerk called him back and demanded the money. He
handed it over and stepped out on to the pavement, his
hands shaking so much as he turned over the pages of
the paper that he could scarcely read the quivering
print. He scanned column after column, his hopes falling, because even though he now felt his report to have
been bad he still hoped against hope that it might have
been printed.

Then suddenly he caught sight of a heading, tucked
away towards the foot of a column:

EXCITING WIN FOR DUMFRIES ACADEMY

He gulped and felt his heart lurch with excitement
and pleasure as he scanned the words he had written.
They looked curiously different in print to what he had

written out in his best handwriting, but they were his words, sure enough.

He rushed back into the office and bought another two copies of the paper and then, his feet hardly seeming to touch the ground, he rushed back to Victoria Terrace to show his brother and his sister his first appearance in print.

9

Writings

Wellwood Anderson began work on his new magazine and James, after much thought, wrote a little article for it which he called *Reckolections of a Schoolmaster: Edited by James Barrie, M.A., A.S.S., LL.D.* It was a humorous article full of intentional misspellings and Wellwood Anderson was very pleased with it, so much so that he asked for more for the next number of *The Clown*.

Wellwood wrote out the pages of *The Clown* in his

own handwriting, eight pages to each issue, and the magazine ran for four issues in each of which some of James's *Reckolections* appeared. After that Wellwood found that it took too much time to write eight closely-packed pages each week and the magazine died.

James continued to write reports on the school cricket matches for *The Dumfries Standard,* and enjoyed the satisfaction of seeing his work in print. But reporting on cricket matches was not so much fun as making up articles of his very own, and he was sorry when *The Clown* ceased publication and wondered if he would ever be able to write proper articles which would be printed.

Besides his writing he found something else to interest him.

On the corner of Shakespeare Street and Queen Street stood the little Theatre Royal. Touring companies of actors came to play here, and once or twice James took his carefully saved pocket money and bought a cheap seat in the pit to watch the performances. He saw much of Shakespeare and the classical dramatists and several more modern plays, but somehow there was something unsatisfactory about sitting at the back of the theatre watching these plays. For some time he was not sure what it was.

True, the companies which played at the Theatre Royal were not the most famous ones. Very rarely were there any actors whose names were well known. The big companies went to places like Edinburgh and Glasgow and scorned the little theatre in Dumfries. James found some of the performances he saw crude and unbelievable. The actors on the whole seemed content to deliver their lines in a rolling, resonant voice which sounded marvellous but meant nothing, and James might have

given up going to the theatre if he had not discovered
what it was that drew him to these performances.

It was the business of actually putting a play on the
stage which fascinated him.

So one evening he went to the box office when a
touring company was presenting *Hamlet.*

The man selling tickets in the box office looked very
much like an actor. His hair was long and he had the
sort of shining face which make-up gives. His gestures
were large and flowery as though he was always giving a
performance on the stage. The foyer of the theatre was
fairly crowded with people going in to watch the performance.

'I want a seat in the front row,' said James.

'My dear sir, all the good seats are sold,' said the man
in a deep resonant voice which would probably have
been happier reciting the blank verse of a Shakespeare
play. 'The company is proving very popular, and there
is not a great choice of seats left –'

'I dinna want a good seat,' said James. 'I want one at
the side. Hae ye got one?'

'A seat at the side in the front row?' said the man in
surprise. No one ever asked for a seat there. You were so
far to the side that half your view of the stage was cut
off. People only bought the side seats when there was
absolutely nothing else to be had. 'I fear the seats at the
side are not good, young sir.'

'But ye hae one?' asked James.

'Oh, certainly, certainly, we have several, in fact. Are
you quite sure that is what you require?'

'Aye,' said James firmly.

The man shrugged. These Scotch yokels had funny
ideas about where they wanted to sit in a theatre. But
then what more could you expect in an uncivilised part

of the world like this? In London, now, people knew
what they were about, and no one who *was* anyone
would think about buying a side seat when there were
better ones available.

'I can give you the last seat on the left in the front
row,' said the man.

'That'll dae me fine,' said James. 'That's just what I
want.'

He paid his money and made his way into the stalls
while the man in the box office shook his head in puzzle-
ment and then turned on his smile again for the next
customer.

James settled himself in his seat and looked round in
satisfaction. There was no one anywhere near him.
Most of the people were gathered in the centre of the
stalls where they would have a good view of the stage
when the play began, but that was not James's idea.

This time in the theatre always gave him a little
thrill. The muted chatter of the audience, the orchestra
gathering in the orchestra pit, tuning up their instru-
ments, the deep warm glow of the gas lamps lighting
the auditorium, and the exciting crimson of the curtain
hiding what was happening in the land of make-believe
beyond. He settled himself comfortably and waited.

The curtain rose on the first scene of *Hamlet*. The
lighting on the stage was dim, but James could make
out a few rostrums set at the back of the stage to represent the battlements of Elsinore Castle. Francisco,
dressed in armour with a spear in his hand, stood in the
middle of the stage looking worried. After a moment
Bernardo came on. The dialogue started and the two
men threw their deep resonant voices at each other and
made big gestures with their arms, rolling their eyes to
show the terror they felt for the ghost which walked

these battlements at night. From his seat so near the
stage James could see that Francisco's finger nails were
chipped and dirty, and Bernardo had a rip in his tights
which had been hastily sewn together with thread of a
slightly different colour.

After a few moments Horatio and Marcellus entered
and the dialogue went on.

But James was not listening to it. On either side, the
stage was edged with tall cut-out pieces of scenery which
prevented most of the audience from seeing off the stage
into the wings, but from where James was sitting he
could see between two of these pieces. He did not watch
the action on the stage at all. He watched what was happening in the wings, supposedly hidden from the
audience's sight. He saw the Ghost of Hamlet's father
stroll towards one of the wing pieces ready to come on
to the stage. He settled his helmet more steadily on his
head, and his fingers pressed the stuck-on beard more
securely against his cheeks. A man in shirt sleeves who
might have been the stage manager had a whispered
conversation with him and James saw the Ghost's metal
helmet glint as the actor playing the part nodded his
head in reply to some question. A minute or two later
the Ghost smoothed down his costume and gave his
beard a final pat as the actor playing Marcellus said:

'Peace! Break thee off; look where it comes again!'

Then the Ghost stalked solemnly on to the stage.
James heard the whisper of surprise and fear go round
the audience, but he himself was not affected by it. He
had seen the Ghost preparing for his entrance and so the
surprise was not there for him.

He found the whole performance fascinating, although he hardly heard a word of what was said on the
stage. The most interesting times of all were after the

scene changes when the curtain went up on a new scene
and James could see the sweating stage hands still man-
handling the scenery they had moved off the stage into
position in the wings where it would be out of everyone's
way. At one time he saw Hamlet and the King come off
the stage after having been quarrelling madly, and they
laughed together and Hamlet slapped the King on the
back as they made their way to a door at the back of the
stage which must have led to the dressing rooms.

To James the most interesting things about the performance did not take place on the stage but in the
wings, where he could watch the workings of the theatre
and see the stage manager and the stage hands doing
the jobs which kept the performance running but which
the audience was not supposed to see.

On the way out after the performance James met a
school friend who had been to see the play too.

'Did ye enjoy it, Jamie?' his friend asked as the
crowd swept past them in the foyer.

'Aye,' said James absently. 'Specially the bit where
Hamlet slapped the King on the back.'

And he walked on, leaving his friend staring after
him with a puzzled look on his face. He could not remember a bit of the play where Hamlet had been on
such friendly terms with Claudius.

*

When Wellwood Anderson asked James to become sec-
retary of the Dramatic Society, James accepted immediately. The thought of joining a club which put on
plays itself was an excellent idea and something which
he had always been keen on, ever since the days when
he had played with the toy theatre in the room above
Mr. Mills's shop in Bank Street.

Amongst James's favourite authors at this time were R. M. Ballantyne whose famous book *The Coral Island* he had read many times, and Fenimore Cooper. Cooper's stories of Red Indians captured his imagination, and in fact it was from one of these stories that James took the plot for his first play written for the Dramatic Society, which he called *Bandelero the Bandit*. It was a short play and it was put on in the Assembly Rooms in Dumfries with two other plays, and James was going to play a part in it himself.

This was a very different matter from the funny little play which he and James Robb had put on in the washhouse at the Tenements. This was the real thing, with a script and lines to learn and moves to be remembered and costumes and make-up to be thought about, and a big audience in the Assembly Rooms to see the finished result. And James was very much older than he had been at that first presentation in the washhouse. He was now sixteen.

The performance was such a success that, despite the protests of a local minister who thought the Academy authorities should be ashamed of themselves for allowing their young men to make fools of themselves on a public platform, it was decided that another programme should be arranged for the next year.

James and Wellwood Anderson worked hard throughout the next winter to prepare another performance by the Dramatic Society. Their time was taken up with rehearsals and play-reading and writing. Wellwood wrote a play for the next season, but James did not. He was too busy rehearsing. There were three short plays to be presented, and he was appearing in two of them. All three were comedies well suited to presentation by schoolboys where if anything went wrong it could be covered up by a laugh or a piece of foolery.

For some ten weeks before the actual performance in the Assembly Rooms the actors were busy finding the right costumes to wear. As James was playing a woman in one of the plays, *The Weavers*, he spent some time looking for a lady's hat to which he could attach false hair, and eventually he found the right thing and wore it proudly at rehearsals after that.

Wellwood produced and stage managed the plays. He never seemed to stop. He could always be seen in the classrooms and corridors of the school, his pockets bulging with prompt copies, lists of properties to be made or borrowed for the plays, and sometimes even the properties themselves. Their schoolwork occasionally suffered because they were thinking too much of the plays, and if a master beat them for not doing their work properly they would look at him scornfully afterwards and say to each other that *he* would never make an actor, but if he were to ask very politely they might be able to find him a job as a walk-on in one of the plays without any lines to say.

Wellwood nearly went mad at the dress rehearsal. Actors appeared in the most outrageous costumes and then refused to alter them in any way because they liked them the way they were and had grown used to rehearsing in them. By threats and pleading and flattery Wellwood managed to get what he wanted in the end, but when the dress rehearsal was finally over he felt exhausted.

'It'll never work,' he said gloomily to James as they trudged away from the Assembly Rooms. There was a strong March gale blowing along the narrow streets of

Dumfries and occasional splatters of rain did not help Wellwood's unhappy mood.

'Och, well, they say a bad dress rehearsal means a good performance,' said James.

'Who dae?'

'I'm not sure, but I've heard a lot of folk say it.'

'Well, I just hope they're right, for nothing could hae been worse than tonight.'

'Thanks very much.'

'Och, not you, Jamie. You were the one thing that kept me sane. You were fine.'

He thought of James on the stage in his hat with the hair attached to it. Because of his small size James made a very good girl, and he had a way of saying comedy lines absolutely seriously which made them funnier than ever. Wellwood had had a lot of trouble with most of the actors who, when they said a funny line, grinned and looked pleased with themselves, which of course spoilt the effect.

They trudged on along the windy streets in silence for a while.

'If Stuart calls me Addle again I'll bash him,' said James fiercely.

'I've told him, Jamie. I've told him a hundred times that the name of your character is Adele, but it doesna make any difference.'

'I ken. He keeps daein' it. I'm beginnin' tae feel like a bad egg.'

Wellwood laughed but James remained serious.

'After all,' he went on, 'he's supposed tae be my husband in the play, so he ought tae ken how tae pronounce my name. Addle!'

'Never mind. None of the audience'll ken how tae pronounce it, either.'

'I hope ye're right, Wellwood.'

'I wonder what we take the trouble for, Jamie, and that's the truth. I get that nervous I sometimes feel it's not worth it. I'll tell ye this. I'll be glad when tomorrow night's over.'

*

The first play, which was a knockabout farce written by Wellwood, went very well. The pupils of the Academy in the audience roared and cheered to see their school friends making fools of themselves on the stage, while parents and friends applauded politely but were not quite sure what the play had really been about.

When the curtain fell the scene was changed for the next play, and James, standing in the wings, felt his stomach turning over as he heard the chatter and laughter from beyond the curtain and realised that in a few minutes he would be out there facing them. It was a strange feeling, not altogether pleasant, and yet not unpleasant. He watched while the furniture was carried on to the stage which was set up to represent the house where James and his husband lived. The boy who was playing the husband came on to the stage and stood beside him in the wings.

James was about to remind him yet again that his name was Adele and not Addle, but one look at Stuart's face warned him not to. He was very pale under his make-up and his hands were shaking uncontrollably. James knew the feeling. Stuart was suffering from a serious dose of stage fright.

They went on to the stage when the set was finished and took their places at the table which was set for breakfast. There was a bright tablecloth – borrowed

from Wellwood's home – on which were plates, cups
and saucers, teapot and milk jug.

As James felt the top of his head he wondered vaguely
if it was right for a woman to be wearing her hat at
breakfast in her own house, but it was too late to do
anything about it now. If he removed his hat he would
remove his hair as well, and would look extremely odd
dressed as a woman with his own short dark hair on top.

A panting and dishevelled Wellwood ran on to the
stage and had a quick look round.

'All right?' he whispered.

James nodded.

'Good luck. The curtain's just going up,' said Wellwood, and dashed back into the wings.

James smiled encouragingly at Stuart at the other
side of the table, but Stuart's eyes seemed a little glazed.
James patted the back of his head once more and felt
the butterflies fluttering madly inside him.

Stuart crossed his legs and assumed an attitude of ease
which would have convinced nobody. He picked up a
cup and saucer but they rattled so much in his shaking
hands that he quickly put them down again.

The curtains parted.

James sat demurely sipping tea, his little finger stick-
ing out in a genteel manner. The audience quietened.

Stuart suddenly turned away from the table in his
chair, but he had not realised that when he crossed his
legs he had caught the edge of the tablecloth between
them. His movement pulled the cloth and all that stood
on it off the table.

There was a tremendous crash of breaking china.
Stuart sat open-mouthed, gazing at the wreckage he had
caused. James felt himself freeze. Here was disaster, and

they had not yet even spoken the first line of the play!
What on earth could he do?

He got to his feet, feeling his knees a little weak, and
crossed behind the table to Stuart, sitting petrified in his
chair. Very carefully, so as not to disturb his hat with
the hair attached to it, he put his arms round Stuart's
neck and in the high-pitched voice he was using for
Adele, he said loudly:

'You clumsy darling!'

The audience roared and cheered, and such a wave of
sympathy and admiration came from them across the
floats that James felt stunned for a moment. In the
wings he could see Wellwood, white-faced, clapping his
hands together, and the audience was applauding too.

'We'll just carry on, Stuart,' whispered James more
calmly than he was feeling. The audience was making
such noise that they could not possibly hear what he
said.

Gracefully he bent down and began to pick up the
shattered remains of the breakfast and put the bits and
pieces back on the table. Whether the disaster so neatly
averted rid Stuart of his stage fright, or whether the
sound of the audience's applause did the job, from then
on he pulled himself together and the rest of the play
went without a hitch.

*

James wrote no more plays while he was at school. His
mind was turning to more serious things, leaving behind
the world of pirates and robbers and Jacobites which
had filled it for so long.

He began work on an immense three-volume novel.

All his spare time was given to working at this masterpiece which eventually reached 100,000 words. He called this novel *A Child of Nature,* and he drew on his knowledge of Dumfries for its background.

When it was finished he packed it up very carefully and sent it off to a publisher in London. Then he sat back to wait impatiently for a verdict. He had great hopes of his novel. It was long and it was serious, just the sort of novel people were buying at that time, and the more he thought about it the more he felt that it was this type of writing he should be trying. He also wanted to write essays of literary criticism. He had read a lot of the modern and older writers in Mr Anderson's shop and library, and he felt there were many things which could be said about them if he could find the knack.

Ahead of him he saw a rosy path of heavy novels and volumes of criticism of other people's work. That was going to be his life.

But the first thing was to get *A Child of Nature* accepted for publication.

The letter from the publisher arrived at Victoria Terrace some weeks later, and James seized it and hurried to his room to open it and read the good news in private. With trembling fingers he tore open the envelope and drew out the sheet of paper inside.

The publisher, the letter said, thought this novel was 'the work of a clever young lady'. James raised his eyebrows at that, but at least the publisher thought the author was clever even if he had got his sex wrong. The publisher then offered to publish the manuscript if the author would pay him a small matter of one hundred pounds.

James sat for a long time without moving on the edge of his bed, the letter dangling between his fingers. After a few minutes he felt in his pockets and eventually produced a sixpence. He looked from the sixpence – all the money he had in the world – to the letter, and then put the sixpence back in his pocket.

Very slowly and regretfully he tore the publisher's letter into four pieces and put them on the fire.

*

James left Dumfries Academy in the summer of 1878 after spending the five happiest years of his life in the town.

He returned to Kirriemuir for the summer holidays before going on to Edinburgh University in the autumn.

He seemed to look at Kirriemuir with new eyes. He had been home for holidays during his time at Dumfries, of course, but now he felt that Dumfries was behind him and Edinburgh had not yet claimed him, and once again Kirriemuir became his home.

Having been away from home for so long he saw the town in a different light. It was still the same place he had always known: the red stone houses strung out along the Gairie Burn, the new Gairie Linen Works with its chimney belching smoke, the new houses growing outwards from the town to make homes for the ever-growing number of workers the mill needed. The Tenements, when he walked past them, seemed changed, but that was only because he no longer lived there and strangers occupied the little house.

But at the same time he felt somewhat separate from the life of the town. It seemed strange to him that while he had been away in Dumfries, gathering a whole lot of new ideas and experiences, people he had known had gone on living the same lives they had always lived without sharing the ideas and experiences he had had. It made him feel in some ways as though he were an intruder and this feeling was made stronger when he had to ask about people he had known and was told that they were dead or married or gone away, as though he ought to have known.

Strathview welcomed him home. The house seemed to have settled now, losing a lot of its raw newness. The creepers were growing up the walls and the garden was well-tended and flourishing.

Within the house the life of the family went on much as usual. Mr Barrie still occupied his desk at the Gairie Linen Works, Margaret and Jane Ann still ran the household, helped by Isabella, Sara and young Margaret who was now sixteen. James slipped easily into the pleasant, familiar, comfortable life.

His mother was pleased to see him home. She was proud of this boy who had done well at school and was now to go on to the university at Edinburgh to take his Master of Arts degree.

But she was disturbed by his continuing desire to become a writer. Formerly she had treated this as something of a joke. She had encouraged him from his earliest days to write and put his thoughts on paper, and now she realised that what she had started merely as a game was becoming a great deal too serious to James for comfort.

The thought of her son becoming a writer was alarming. She had no knowledge of writers, apart from the few local people who occasionally wrote verses for one of the local papers, but they only wrote in their spare time and had other jobs to keep them and their families. She knew that they were paid little or nothing for what they had printed. It might be that important writers in London were paid well enough for their work, but London was many miles away, a foreign country to Margaret Ogilvy.

'Could ye not become a teacher, Jamie?' she asked one evening as they sat in the living room with the westering sun streaming through the windows. She was sewing a new frill to the sleeve of an old dress. Although she no longer needed to remake old clothes as she had had to do in the old days, the habit died hard, and she would not think of throwing out a dress just because it needed a new frill at the sleeve. 'Alexander is daein' very well,' she went on, 'and you're as clever as he is.'

'I dinna want tae be a teacher, Mother,' James said patiently. 'I want tae be a writer.'

'But if ye were a teacher ye could write in your spare time, could ye not?'

She looked anxiously at him as he sat sprawled in a chair with his feet on the fender.

'There wouldna be enough spare time tae write if I became a teacher,' said James.

'It's not that I want tae stop ye, laddie,' said Margaret. 'It's just that teachin' seems a – a *safer* job than writin'.'

'Ye can make a lot of money at writin'. People are aye wantin' new novels tae read and volumes of essays and things. That's what I want tae dae.'

Margaret sighed. She realised there was no point in trying to persuade James, and she could only hope that during his time at the university he might change his mind.

James spent a happy summer in Kirriemuir, fishing with his old friends, going for long walks round the well-remembered countryside, chatting with the family in the big living room at Strathview.

At the end of October he left Kirriemuir once again, heading this time for Edinbugh and the university, still determined that he was going to become a serious writer of three volume novels and essays.

Postscript

All through his time at Edinburgh University James worked on the idea of writing heavy literary essays and long novels.

He never succeeded at either.

In fact he had a hard time starting on any kind of literary career. Jane Ann showed him a paper with an advertisement for a leader-writer on *The Nottingham Journal,* and without having any very clear idea of what a leader-writer was, James applied for the job and got it. After a spell in Nottingham he moved to London, determined to make his name in the big city. This frightened Margaret Ogilvy, for she thought of London as a huge monster which devoured young men. For a long time James had no success at all, and he lived mainly on penny buns and cups of tea, while he pestered editors and publishers with a constant string of articles, all of which were rejected. Then suddenly an editor accepted an article. It was one he had written mainly for relaxation and it dealt with the life of the Auld Licht Church in Kirriemuir, and from then on his climb to fame started. The public loved the article and demanded more. He wrote more, drawing on all his mother's old stories which he had heard as a child, and when he had used all these Margaret had to keep searching her memory for more incidents to send to her famous son who was taking London by storm.

A great deal of what he wrote we can trace back to his childhood in one way or another. His first published volume of his mother's stories, *Auld Licht Idylls*, are told by an old schoolmaster – could this be the schoolmaster whose 'Reckolections' had originally appeared in *The Clown*? Then came the book which was to bring him international fame, *A Window in Thrums*. This tells the story of a crippled woman who sits at her window and watches the life of the little Scottish weaving town go by her. The town is quite clearly Kirriemuir, and who else is the crippled woman but Bell Lunan? Although there is a little cottage almost opposite Strathview in Kirriemuir which claims to be the original Window in Thrums, many local people believe the real window is the one in Bell Lunan's house which still stands next to the Tenements in the Brechin Road.

Even later when he abandoned this kind of writing for the theatre, we can still trace childhood memories in the plots of his plays. In *Quality Street* the scene is set in a small school run by two maiden ladies. The Hanky School and the Misses Adam must have been clearly in his mind. And his most famous work of all, *Peter Pan*, is full of his old boyhood escapades of playing pirates at Moat Brae in Dumfries. Wendy's house in the trees, built for her by the Lost Boys, is, on the author's own admission, the washhouse behind the Tenements in Kirriemuir.

The Barrie house in the Tenements and the washhouse are open to the public, and in the upstairs room are two of the original hair-bottomed chairs brought into the house on the day James was born.

Honours were showered upon him. In 1913 he was made a baronet and the Order of Merit was conferred on him in 1922. So successful was he as a playwright that at one time he had five plays running in London at the same time. This was not surprising, because he was one of the greatest masters of the craft of writing for the stage there has ever been. Probably this mastery started when he sat in the side seat in the front row of the Theatre Royal in Dumfries and watched the actors and stage hands in the wings.

In 1895 Jane Ann, worn out by continually looking after her ailing mother, died. Margaret Ogilvy followed her three days later. James was quite broken up by this double tragedy. His father died in 1902 in his 88th year, and then only as the result of an accident.

Sir James Barrie died on 19th June 1937 at the age of 77, and five days later he was buried in the family grave at Kirriemuir. On the headstone, under the names of his mother, of his sister Jane Ann, of the two little sisters he had never known, Elizabeth and Agnes, of his brother David who died so tragically, and of his father, is inscribed the simple epitaph of the great dramatist:

JAMES MATTHEW BARRIE. 1860–1937.